THE CRASH

Alison Butler Robinson

Published in the United States of America

ISBN: 9798394807923

The many crashes in life, along with the devastating events that brought me to my Savior.

In memory of my sweet daughter, Brooke Maree Butler, who I made a promise to—that I would never quit telling her story, and how we have a wonderful Redeemer to carry us through.

Dedication

I dedicate this book to my beautiful children and my husband, as they walk with me hand and hand through this journey called life.

I also dedicate this book to my sweet friend, Charla Turner, who inspired me to start writing. Thank you for being a lifelong friend.

How I Survived

CHAPTER 1

As the Journey Begins…

It's November 16, 2017. The day I decided to start writing my story. It's also the day I married my first husband, twenty-one rollercoaster years ago.

My faith has led me to write with the desire of helping others. I believe so many people can relate to my experiences and gain inspiration from what I have to share. Even those who can't, I hope you will be touched by my journey.

A little bit about myself… I'm just a small-town girl, born in Georgia and raised there in a Christian home out in the country. Full of imperfections. Some would call me a true "Georgia Peach." Brought up in a Baptist church, I attended both Christian and public schools. I married right out of high school and had three beautiful children by the time I was twenty-five.

My firstborn was a beautiful little girl we named Brooke. My second born, also my first son, we called Jacob. My third child, Wyatt, also a boy, was the baby for many years. Growing up, I always wanted to be a wife and a mother, a role I loved and cherished.

After Brooke was born, I enrolled in cosmetology school. My young husband started his own business, which caused him to work out of town a lot. Of course, marriage isn't easy—it takes a lot of work and compromise. And fresh out of high school, even more. We were still growing up.

Sadly, after twelve years of marriage, our relationship ended in a divorce. Something I promised myself would never happen. I *loved* my husband. I *prayed* for my marriage. I gave it *many* chances, in hopes things would change. The one thing I said "never" to came to reality. We tried to reconcile, we went to Christian counseling, and again, I prayed a lot. But God did not lead me to go back. It was one of the hardest things I've ever had to experience.

Early in my marriage, I faced many fears. Being a new mother could be scary at times, though something I always wanted. Even as a child, I dreamt about becoming a mom and having a big family. But I suppose, when you love so deeply, it was only natural I faced fears with every single one of my children in some way.

I remember, like yesterday, finding out I was pregnant at the young age of nineteen. Making the phone call to get my results. For a little while, I sensed something just wasn't right. My body felt off in some way. I took two pregnancy tests. Both read negative, but the blood test came back positive. When I called to get those results and heard the word "positive," my life instantly changed forever in that moment.

For the better, in so many ways. Becoming a mother brought me closer to my Lord and Savior, Jesus. For several days, I walked around in shock. The reality I carried a baby inside of me was surreal. I was going to be *a mom*! Something I always dreamed of. Little did I know, the journey would not be easy, or the happy fairytale I expected.

Carrying my first child proved scary at times and often overwhelming. Nausea plagued me throughout my pregnancy. I lost weight in the beginning, instead of gaining it, and I was so sick—

morning, noon, and night. I just tried to keep my eyes on the end result—my sweet little precious angel growing inside of me that would change my life for the better.

Naturally, when we received the news that something was wrong, it scared me to death. I remember being at the doctor's office, monitoring the baby through several ultrasounds, which resulted in sending me to a specialist. I waited for what felt like hours for the results. They returned to tell me that I had a two-vessel umbilical cord when it should be three. It is also referred to as having a "single umbilical artery." The specialist told me so many things I couldn't process them all at the young age of nineteen. They advised her kidneys could be affected, and her head might be larger than her body, but in time it would all catch up. I just cried and cried for days, praying that everything would be okay. I eventually found peace, and the will to enjoy the rest of my pregnancy. So the night came when it was time to deliver this sweet precious gift God had given us.

I will never forget the night of May 3. The day before I walked on my mom's treadmill in hopes it would induce labor. As the night went on, contractions started, but nothing consistent. It grew later in the evening and by midnight, I lost what they call your lovely "mucus plug." *Could this really be happening?* We laid down to watch a movie, in hopes I would keep progressing. It was storming and pouring down rain outside. The movie ended at around three a.m. and still nothing consistent. I decided at that point we should just go to sleep.

As I was getting ready to slide into bed, something happened. I looked at my husband and said, "My water just broke."

He looked at me and said, "Are you sure you didn't just wet your pants?"

Keep in mind, it was late, we were tired, and we had been to the hospital two other times with false labor. I proceeded to get up and call my midwife, Marcia. She instructed me to go ahead and get to the hospital. We grabbed our things on that rainy night and rushed off to the labor and delivery ward.

Shortly after we arrived, I was checked, and sure enough, my water had broken. My amazing little girl would be arriving soon. She proved to be the hardest labor. At one point, I literally looked at my midwife and told her I was going to die. I said, "I am not going to make it through this." Keep in mind, this was after ten hours of Pitocin and not even reaching four centimeters, without an epidural yet. Finally, the time came when I could receive one, after begging for what seemed like hours.

In the meantime, a news crew, Channel 46, showed up at the hospital. I remember being in so much pain, and my husband informing them it was totally fine to come in. *What in the world?* Come to find out, they were doing a story on midwives—and by the way, mine was amazing! Marcia, my midwife, had told them that we would be a great couple for the story. As you read on, you will see there is never a dull moment in my life. Little did I know at the time, God always had a plan and the news crew was obviously part of it...

So here I was, in so much pain, surrounded by my family, my friends, my husband, my midwife, and a news crew. There were actually only two Channel 46 people in the room—a cameraman and a sweet lady named April Nelson. She would be the one covering the story. This was just my first incident on the news, with several more to come. The cameraman was having a hard time, bless his heart.

My mother-in-law found him out in the hallway, leaning his head against the wall, looking so distraught. She proceeded to ask him, "Sir, are you okay?"

He replied, "Oh, yes ma'am, but she is in so much pain and there is nothing they can do for her."

About an hour after getting my epidural, it finally kicked in. I was in heaven! Only about thirty minutes went by and it was time to push.

Everyone left the room except my husband, the hospital staff, my midwife, April Nelson, and of course the respectful camera man who faced the window the entire time. After about an hour of pushing, we welcomed my sweet little angel into this big world. She was bright-eyed and beautiful and started life with her first appearance on the news.

CHAPTER 2

The Motherhood Journey Begins…

The instant I laid eyes on my sweet baby girl, my life was forever changed. We named her Brooke Maree. She was absolutely perfect! Her kidneys worked fine, and her body and head were proportioned. Praise God!!! All the many prayers from family, loved ones, and friends worked. This sweet little green-eyed, brown curly-headed girl changed my life for the better. My life was no longer about me—it was about my family.

Becoming a mother brought me closer to God. At the time Brooke was born, we were living in the basement of my in-law's home. I have so many memories there. Looking back, I learned so much from my mother-in-law. She taught me how to cook, and she is one of the many reasons I love being in the kitchen today. I call it my happy place.

Shortly after Brooke was born, I decided to go to cosmetology school. My husband worked full-time, while also earning a degree in fiber optics and telecommunications. When I graduated, Brooke was two years old, and we were able to buy our own home. Oh, how I loved that little house. It was an old shotgun house built in 1908 that had been added on to three times. Definitely a fixer-upper, so we added our finishing touches to it with love and prayer and called it home.

That house holds so many memories. Some sad, some happy, and some wild. It would take about five books to tell you all the things that happened there. When I say my life has never been boring, and never a dull moment, I mean it. For instance, we had a little bit of land there, so with that came field mice. If you have ever lived out in the country, you know the little critters I am talking about. And if you do, you also know why it is always good to have a cat. My husband hated possums and rats. I really don't know of anyone who likes them. So one day, as I looked out the kitchen window just admiring him cutting the grass, I noticed his pistol on his side. Every once in a while I would hear a *pow-pow* and know he just killed a rat in the field.

We had nine-foot ceilings in our home, and one time we had bats literally fly in, circling around the ceiling. As you can imagine, some rather hilarious antics ensued. Oh, I wish I could have been a fly on the wall that night. Those suckers weren't easy to get out either and liked to return. I even had a friend come over one time to help us with them. We made the best of it, though, and built a family of five there.

When Brooke was a little over two, I was ready for another baby. I wanted another little one running around. My husband and I discussed it and started trying. However, conceiving did not happen right away—it took almost a year. Every month, I took a test, and every month I found myself disappointed when it did not read positive. If there's one thing I can share with you that I have learned throughout my life, it is this—God's timing is not our timing, but it is the best timing of all.

He knows what is best for our lives, although so many times, we think that we do. If we could just understand and trust Him at all times, it would save us from so much disappointment.

CHAPTER 3

Stepping Into Motherhood…

When Brooke was one, she started running a really high fever. We took her to the doctor, and they ran some tests. It took a few days to get the results. I received a call stating that Brooke had E. Coli, and also a bladder infection. Bless her heart… She couldn't tell us what was going on as a one year old. Her urine had stayed in her bladder for so long, the bacteria turned to E. Coli.

Something was going on with her kidneys, so we were referred to a urologist. She had to go through testing every year to monitor what was called "reflux of the kidneys." Brooke's urine would go back up into both kidneys instead of emptying. In some cases, it only happens to one kidney.

So what did we do? We poured our hearts into prayer. The tests she had to do were heartbreaking. She would be on antibiotics until age three and back and forth for follow-up testing every year. As a mother, watching your child go through something uncontrollable is heartache. Little did I know, as a new mom, that this was the hardest part of being a mom… And so, such pain would also be a part of the rest of my life. Because reality is, nothing is really in our control, even if you are a Christ follower.

When Brooke turned two, we went for her yearly testing. After many, many prayers, Brooke's reflux in one kidney remained. The other had completely healed. Thank you, Jesus! When Brooke turned three, we yet again returned for her yearly testing, and praise God, it was gone. She was healed! No more reflux! We were so happy little Brookie was okay.

As we entered the next chapter in our lives with having another baby, I decided to do things a little differently. I didn't want to find out the sex of the baby. I wanted it to be a surprise. Now my husband, on the other hand, was not so excited about that decision. I remember praying, asking God to please let me have a baby boy that looked just like his daddy. With Brooke, I basically had a clone of myself.

Throughout this pregnancy, I grew closer to God. Reading His word daily and trusting Him that everything would go smoothly with this pregnancy.

Let me tell a funny little story about my husband. He could not control himself. The suspense of not knowing if we were going to have a boy or a girl was killing him. One day he called the doctor without me knowing, and when I went for my appointment they said, "Your husband called and asked us the sex of the baby." They simply told him, "Mr. Butler, I promise, you will not be disappointed either way." We laughed so hard about that. He thought he was going to be sneaky!

This pregnancy, like all of mine, proved unique. No sickness this time, and for the most part, things went very well. I was reading the Bible one day and ran across a verse in Genesis. The story of Rebekah, who could not have children. God blessed her and she became pregnant with twins. I used to always say I would love to have a girl and twin boys one day. God blessed Rebekah, and she became pregnant with twin boys named Esau and Jacob. I told myself that day, if I had a son, I would name him Jacob.

We started preparing for this little one to enter the world. Now that we owned our own home, the baby would get a room, and of course, that was our next project. We did the nursery in Noah's ark. Back then, stenciling was a big thing, so I stenciled Noah's Ark and animals all over the room. I also painted a verse on one of his walls that I have gone back to many times throughout my life. Proverbs 22:6, *Train up a child in the way he should go; and when he is old, he will not depart from it.* This verse is so true.

My father would go outside at night. He told me that was his alone time with God, a time to pray and talk to Him. I know he prayed for me daily growing up, and he raised me in the way I should go. He guided me on how to live as a Christian.

So many times I veered off that path. What some people would call "backsliding." For me, it was doing things my way, but I was always brought back to the place of righteousness, humbleness, love, and discipline. As Christians, I believe God only lets us go so far, but He always brings us back to Him out of love and discipline. God loves us so much. He does it for our own good. He does not want to see His children suffer, and many times, when I did things my way, that is what it brought me to—suffering. He always saved me though. God protects us in times when we don't even see it, or have a clue that He is doing so.

We finished the nursery, and since I didn't know if I was having a boy or a girl, I stuck with primary colors. I remember purchasing plaid bedding. In the back of my mind, my gut was telling me it was a boy, seeing how things seemed so different with this pregnancy. I could just picture him—holding him and calling him Jacob. I did have a girl name picked out too—Hannah Leigh. Leigh after my father and I.

I prayed over my belly, asking God to use this child in ministry one day. I remember being so happy. My pregnancy was going great.

Any sickness ended after the first trimester, unlike my pregnancy with Brooke. Then one night, I woke up out of my sleep in the middle of the night, and could not move. I felt paralyzed. A dreadful fear washed over me like nothing I ever felt before. I could not even speak. When I opened my eyes, something hovered right in my face. Have you ever been somewhere and you could sense someone looking at you, and when you look their way, they actually were? That is exactly how I felt…but there was no one there. It was dark, a black presence over my body, like a shadow.

I used to keep the light on in the bathroom, so it would shine in my room. I fixated on this evil feeling all around me. I could not speak, could not move. Fear overwhelmed me. All I could do was exactly what I was taught to do—pray and rebuke. So in my mind, I recited, "I rebuke you in the name of Jesus! Get behind me, Satan!" Whatever this was around me, it was trying to take something from me. As I type this, the verse just came to me. It is found in John 10:10, *The thief comes only to steal, kill and destroy; I have come that they may have life, and have it to the full.*

I then looked up at the ceiling in the corner of my room, and a bright light, brighter than the bathroom light, glared in my room. Now I wasn't just rebuking in my mind, I was able to whisper it. As I kept rebuking, the fear finally lifted and the shadow retreated. The next day when I woke, I knew it had not been a dream. I went about my daily duties as a mother and a wife. I knew I'd had a spiritual encounter, but crazy as it sounded, I put it in the back of my mind.

I told myself with this pregnancy, I was going to make sure I was in labor. I would not take a hundred trips to the hospital for them to send me home.

On September 27, 2000 I started having labor pains. I determined I would wait it out, until absolutely positive this was labor. As the night went on, the contractions came closer and closer together. At around five in the morning, I decided to wake my husband and tell him we needed to head to the hospital. I didn't want to go too early, but I definitely didn't want to wait until too late. After meeting my mother-in-law and dropping Brooke off, we headed to the hospital. So guess what? We drove all the way to the hospital…and my contractions stopped. They stopped! Little did I know at the time, this was the grace of God. I went straight to the bathroom and started doing squats. I was saying to myself, "Come on! Let's do this!" And to the baby, "I know you are ready to see the world, and we are so ready to meet you!"

I was trying to do things my way. You know, be in control of the situation? Shortly after that, for the first time, I experienced what it felt like for my life to be so far out of my control.

I was placed in a temporary room with curtains and put on monitors to see if I actually was in labor. If I showed signs of labor, then I would be placed in a delivery room. I will never forget the sound of the machine that monitors the baby's heart rate. Still to this day, when I hear it, I develop anxiety.

I commented to my husband, "That sounds very slow." If you've heard a baby's heartbeat before, you know it usually sounds very fast. I started thinking maybe they messed up, and I was hearing my heart beating and not the baby's.

I asked my husband what the number on the monitor was. He replied, "Fifty."

Surely not the baby's. There must be a mix-up. The nurse came back and started moving the monitor around. She never said a word about anything or what was going on. When she left the room, I again asked my husband what the number was on the monitor. He replied, "Fifty…now it's zero."

My heartrate skyrocketed, anxiety flooding in like a tidal wave. Something wasn't right. I inhaled a deep breath, trying to calm myself, and then all of a sudden the nurse who was monitoring us, along with four other nurses, rushed into my room.

From there, everything happened so fast. They dropped the top of my bed, so my head was slanted downward.

They placed me on oxygen for the baby and had me drink something—I have no idea what it was—and started an IV as fast as they could. I went into shock. I couldn't think. Again, I experienced this overwhelming feeling as if something was trying to take something from me. When they would ask me a question, I would just look at my husband, because I could not answer. I sought him for the answer, and he could see what was going on. He answered every question for me.

I heard my doctor's voice as he entered the room. He seemed so calm and in control, which helped me settle down some. He looked at me and said, "Alison, I am going to have your baby out in three minutes." The nurses threw my husband some scrubs and instructed him to go put them on, knowing he would not be able to return due to the circumstances. I watched him grab the garments and leave. They rushed me to the operating room, where my doctor was already scrubbing in—to get the baby out. I looked up at the anesthesiologist, who said to me, "Everything is going to be okay. You are going to go to sleep now," and out I went.

So you could say this delivery definitely did not go as planned. I pictured this day being so exciting—watching my husband's face when the doctor announced if it was a boy or a girl. My husband cutting the cord. The doctor placing my sweet bundled baby in my arms.

Oh, I had it all planned out. I even intended to attempt this labor completely naturally, with no epidural or any pain meds.

So long I'd dreamt of the look on my husband's face. The surprise and joy when we welcomed our baby and learned if it were a boy or girl.

Isn't it funny how when we try to plan things *our* way, much of the time it does not turn out that way?

So yet again my plans went array. I've experienced the taste of disappointment, the letdown of the messiness of life many times, thinking matters would be one way, only to be so disenchanted.

In Jeremiah 29:11, *God says, "For I know the plans I have for you, declares the Lord. Plans to prosper you and not to harm you, plans to give you hope and a future."* Looking back, my contractions stopping when I arrived at the hospital proved to be His loving grace. He knew the outcome, He heard all of my prayers, and He protected us both from danger. He would not let the enemy have His way.

After surgery, they moved me to the recovery room. As I awoke, the only thing on my mind, as groggy as I felt, was *Is my baby okay?* I asked the nurse sitting next to me, and she replied, "Your baby is fine. You had a little boy."

A sigh of relief came over me, and I allowed myself to rest. My husband's first name was Michael, so we named him Michael Jacob, but we called him Jacob. He was such a precious baby and looked just like his father. Just as I had asked for.

How vividly I remember the day we brought him home and placed him in the cradle. My sweet little Brookie just loved him so much. She could not stop talking. So excited. I remember walking by my room and looking in. She was just swinging the cradle back and forth, a little too fast, just singing her little heart out. Those beautiful brown curls that reminded me of Shirley Temple, and that sweet little voice, I will never forget.

CHAPTER 4

When the Panic and Anxiety Started

One morning, *I* woke as usual and started doing laundry. Dustin was home from work that day. My laundry room was right outside of Jacob's room. I peeked my head in to check on him. As I started to close the door, low and behold, a snake slithered across the floor. In today's terms, I would have said "Not Today Satan."

I went to wake Dustin. He went and captured the snake and killed it. The odd thing was Dustin could not identify this snake. He had pet snakes as a kid and was very knowledgeable about them.

My mind immediately went back to all the incidents with Jacob. In my mind, I protested. *You are not taking him from me. He is a child of God.*

I began to pray and rebuke. I believe Jacob has a great calling on his life. I pray that he keeps his eyes on Jesus and that he follows where God leads him. I pray that he fulfills his calling. I believe that is the only way for us as Christians to find happiness.

In 2 Thessalonians 1:11-12, the Bible says, *With this in mind we constantly pray for you, that our God may make you worthy of His calling, and by*

His power, He may bring to fruition your every desire for goodness and your every deed prompted by faith. Lord Jesus may be glorified in you, and you in Him, according to the grace of our God and the Lord Jesus Christ.

After having Jacob in the hospital, I suffered my first panic attack. If you've ever had one, you understand they are terrible. I literally worried I was dying. All at once, I felt scared, overwhelmed, anxious, and light-headed. My chest felt heavy. My mind spun out of control. All the medication of having an emergency C-section and my hormones being way off balance contributed.

That first panic attack ushered in another period in my life that spiraled completely out of my control. I could not manage the situation no matter how much I wanted to fix it. The panic attacks kept coming. I had loved ones praying for me. I prayed constantly. Yet, for the first week we were home, this continued. I would fall asleep and wake up in terror, look at the clock, and it'd only been two minutes.

I finally just pictured in my head Jesus holding me. Cradling me like a baby, and I slept like one. I went back to scripture where the Bible says in Isaiah 41:10, *Fear not, for I am with you, be not dismayed, for I am your God. I will strengthen you, I will uphold you with my righteous right hand.* When the second week passed, the anxiety lifted.

So here we were, this little family of four. A little girl, one I thought of as an angel, and a little boy cute as a button. When Jacob was four months, I started feeling unwell. Something was off. I knew my body…and something just did not feel right. But surely I wasn't pregnant again. Not so soon.

I called Dustin and explained that I didn't know what in the world was wrong. I just didn't feel right. I had a friend who volunteered at a pregnancy center. She offered, "Run by here and take a pregnancy test the next time you are out. You're probably not though—you're probably just tired from having two little ones instead of one."

The entire ride there I was determined there was no way I could be pregnant again. Why was I even doing this? When I arrived, the sweet lady said, "Come on in. I'll be right with you and you can go take your test."

I took the test and then I had to wait in another room for the results. I remember thinking it was probably taking so long because it was negative. Of course it was! The sweet lady came back out and said, "Well, honey, it's positive."

"Really?" I responded. A smile lit my face right before I went into shock.

They were so kind. They encouraged me to watch videos and gave me a nice gift basket. I was still in shock. All I could say was, "Oh thank you, but this is my third baby."

A short while later, I slid into my car. *Is this really happening so soon?* I always wanted a girl and twin boys, so I guess this was the closest thing to having twins, seeing how these babies would be fourteen months apart.

I am a very take-charge kind of person. I like always having a plan in place. To me, making sure things are taken care of and lined up is a good thing. I think it's a natural part of being a mother, always wanting to make sure everything is going to be okay. Trying to fix things. Always trying to see the positive.

It was time to call my husband.

I reached him on the phone and blurted out the exciting news.

Naturally, his reaction was, "WHAT? You're kidding me, right?"

I said, laughing, "Well, it's all your fault."

My positive side determined everything would be okay. Perhaps it would be another boy. The two could share a room. Perhaps even share clothes. They would be best friends.

By the end of the day, as evening settled in and the day winded down, the realization started to set in. The tears came. I didn't want to go to the doctor every month. I didn't want another C-section.

What if my postpartum anxiety set in again? What if there were even more complications to this pregnancy? What if it were too soon for my body?

I called my dad, crying, and he encouraged me, "Now, Alison, everything is going to be fine."

That was always his answer. I don't remember ever seeing my dad really stressed out or out of sorts. If he was, he had a pretty calm way of showing it. It seemed he took everything in steady stride...and prayer. I am sure as soon as we hung up the phone he went to God.

As I pictured him doing so, God reminded me that *His plans* are not always *our plans*—and His plans are always greater. There's the verse in the Bible—Isaiah 55: 8-9. *"For my thoughts are not your thoughts, neither are your ways my ways," declares the Lord. "As the heavens are higher than the earth, so are my ways higher than your ways and my thoughts than your thoughts."*

Children are truly a gift from God. As I said from the beginning, having my firstborn changed me for the better, and so would having my third. By the end of the night, we were laughing about it and growing excited. We put prayer into action very early that there would be no anxiety and no C-section. We also decided we would find out the sex of this baby. I couldn't put Dustin through that again. When the time came, we learned we were indeed going to have another little boy.

This time, I suggested Dustin should come up with the name. He started coming up with some names like Henry and Remington. Yikes! I decided maybe I should offer a few suggestions to guide him along. He obviously liked guns and country names. So one day I said, "What do you think about Wyatt?"

He thought a minute and answered, "Yes, that's it. Wyatt is an awesome name."

We settled on Dustin Wyatt, and he would go by Wyatt. Both of my boys were named after their father.

Chapter 5

Never a Dull Moment...

Nine months went by pretty fast with two little ones and one on the way. There were doctor's appointments for me every month and all the well visits for an infant the first year. Brookie enrolled in tap and ballet. We were a busy little family trying to make ends meet.

We'd become members of a little church called Union Grove Baptist. That's where my little Brookie eventually came to know her Lord and Savior while attending Vacation Bible School. She was six years old, the same age as I when I became saved. I'll never forget her telling me as we were driving home one night that she'd asked Jesus to come into her heart. That was one special day. My heart was overjoyed and filled with emotion.

How quickly time went by. Nine months came to an end, and I was off to the hospital again. With the circumstances with Brooke and Jacob, they considered me high-risk and instructed me not to wait around at home this time. As soon as I started to feel the signs of labor, I should come to the hospital. So that is exactly what we did. I hoped to have a natural birth with this baby as well—at least that was my plan. No pain medication, no epidural, and hopefully no C-section. All the medication from my last delivery likely contributed to the panic and anxiety.

When I arrived at the hospital, I was three centimeters, almost four. I had never shown that much progression before reaching the hospital. I was so happy. Maybe things would go as hoped after all!

Things moved right along. I remained adamant I wanted no medication unless necessary. Things started getting tough, the pain really set in, unbearable at times. I remained determined to manage this delivery naturally. I am the type of person who once I set my mind to do something, there is no turning back... I do it.

All of a sudden, machines started going off. I didn't know what was happening. The nurse ran into my room and announced that the baby was in distress and going into cardiac arrest. She strapped oxygen on me and lowered the top of my bed.

It was happening again.

Immediately, I began praying. All I could think of was 2 Corinthians 5:7—*Walk by faith, not by sight.* That means to live believing in the unseen, not what you can see. Suddenly his heart rate leveled out.

My doctor rushed into the room to check on me. "Alison, I think you need to go ahead and get an epidural for the baby's sake, just in case we have to do a C-section."

As devastated and scared as I was, of course I wanted to do what was best for the baby. I received the epidural. They placed an internal monitor on the baby to monitor his heartbeat.

As time passed and things progressed, I grew very uncomfortable. I noticed the epidural was not working as well. They called the anesthesiologist back in so he could make sure I was comfortable. Time went by—something did not seem right. My chest started to feel numb and so did my face. I didn't say a word as I started to panic. I reached up and wiggled my nose, and I could not feel it.

In a daze, I stared at everyone in the room—my mom, my sister, Dustin, Dustin's mom, and Dustin's grandmother. I sat straight up and said, "The epidural is going the wrong way!" in a frantic voice. "I can't feel my face!" All of a sudden, things turned a little crazy. I began throwing up and could not stop. My body felt so weird. The internal monitor flat-lined. I grabbed the oxygen mask and started sucking in oxygen as fast as I could, thinking the baby was getting none. Then I started throwing up again.

All of a sudden I felt movement in my birth canal. I had been leaning off of the bed, throwing up into a trash can. I quickly laid on my back. The nurse came running in. I threw the covers off and said, "Check me, check me now."

Sure enough, Wyatt had halfway entered the world. His eyes were wide open. Everyone ran out of the room in a hurry. I will never forget my sister's face. A priceless expression, her eyes huge. She left the room saying, "That's not supposed to happen, is it?"

The nurse looked at me. I said to her, "I know you want me to wait to push until the doctor gets here. I'm sorry, but this baby is coming out now."

And he did. Dustin Wyatt Butler entered the world with no doctor even in the room. Having two other children, I'd experienced all the stages of childbirth, but I could not wrap my head around going through it like this. I'd already entered the transition stage where the baby was moving down the birth canal. What does your body do when you throw up? You push! As I was vomiting, my body was thrusting him out. When I leaned back on the bed, I became aware.

Like I said, never a dull moment! Another pregnancy that definitely didn't go as planned. I could hear my doctor whistling as he came down the hall—the same doctor who was so calm while delivering Jacob.

Gratefulness overwhelmed me. Wyatt was healthy and a C-section hadn't been necessary. I thanked Jesus for His many blessings again. Things might not always go as planned or predicted, but His way is always the best way. Always.

So here we were, a family of five as I had always wanted. One girl and two boys. Life appeared grand, although a lot of responsibility rested on our shoulders at the young age of twenty-four.

I started working at a salon called Trendsetters a couple of days a week, as well as doing hair out of my home so I could be present with the kids. My husband's work often obligated him to travel several hours, so he would rent an apartment and stay throughout the week and come home on the weekends. I felt as though I was raising three kids on my own. Life grew painfully lonely. Little did I know, my marriage was falling apart. Things started to change. The distance between us amplified. A year went by of feeling this way. It was devastating. I starved for attention from my husband, but he wasn't there. Even when home, it was as if he were still gone.

CHAPTER 6

Life Takes a Drastic Turn

A year passed, and I turned twenty-five. The morning started with getting Brookie off to school, then I just had the two boys at home with me. I had laundry to do, then it was off to the grocery store. I started running a bath to get them ready for the day. Wyatt was almost one and Jacob had just recently turned two.

Wyatt had a little bath seat with suction cups on the bottom. I preferred to use that for him because he could play and be safe. I sat Jacob in the tub and ran the water just enough to cover their legs—only a couple of inches. Then I discovered that I had no towels in the bathroom. Earlier that morning, I'd hauled them all to the back of the house to wash. Never did it cross my mind that anything could happen in the short span it took me to dash to the back of the house.

When I returned, I found Wyatt was out of his bath seat. Floating face down, lifeless—Jacob still playing as if nothing was even going on. My heart bolted. I grabbed him as fast as I could. I will never forget his little face—his eyes rolled back in his head, his lips blue. Did he even have a heartbeat? I grabbed the phone and called 911. When the dispatcher answered, all I could say was, "My baby has drowned." Panic consumed me, and I fought to think straight. I remembered learning infant CPR as a teenager when I briefly worked for a daycare. I told the dispatcher I was going to start CPR. I laid his lifeless body down but first I spoke to God and begged, "God PLEASE don't take my baby!"

As I started to breathe in his mouth, his lips turned pink again. He remained unconscious, his little belly so full of water from drinking it. I started chest compressions and did not see any improvement. I transitioned to something that I would do if one of my children were choking. I sat him up and rubbed the center of his back. When I leaned him back over he opened his eyes, looked at me, and said, "Momma." I knew at that point oxygen had not been cut off too long because he was alert and recognized me. He was breathing fine. His coloring returned. While all of this was going on, I'd laid the phone down. I grabbed it and the dispatcher said, "I heard everything. Good job."

Shock engulfed me. I don't even remember giving her my address. Stunned, I walked in the living room and watched the ambulance pass my house. I informed her they missed us.

The house flooded with EMTs and firemen. They listened to Wyatt and checked his vitals. They told me that they didn't even hear water in his lungs. I recognized then it was a miracle from God. My eyes filled up with tears and all I could say was, "Thank you, Jesus. Thank you!"

Wyatt seemed very tired, although that was understandable. He would usually take a nap at that time and he also had put up a fight, wrestling with the water to stay alive. Since he responded more to me than to the EMTs, they decided to life-flight him as a precaution.

I could not ride in the helicopter and needed to drive myself to the hospital. I phoned my mom for help, and she agreed to come pick up Jacob and also Brooke from school. Then I called a sweet friend of mine who made it to my house in no time. She rode with me to the hospital.

By the time she made it over, I was spinning circles in my house. I didn't know what to do, what to take, or where I was going. I could not shake the utter shock. I'm so glad I had my friend with me. My mind constantly danced around the worst-case scenarios—what if something happened to him on the way there and I wasn't with him? What if he was scared, crying, or wanting his mom? What sort of stress was that causing his heart?

Then my mind went to Dustin. What was he going to think? Would he think I was a terrible mother? Irresponsible? I hadn't even called him yet.

The thoughts wouldn't stop. My mind raced out of control. I contacted Dustin to let him know. He was actually working not far from the hospital and immediately called his dad, who was right near the hospital. He even saw the helicopter land. I was so thankful Wyatt would have a familiar face when he arrived.

The drive was a blur. I even had to stop and get gas. All I wanted was to hold my baby.

When I finally arrived, they took me to his room. When I walked in there, Dustin held Wyatt. The doctor looked at me and said, "So I hear you did a great job bringing him back around." I sighed in relief. But I know it was God, not me. I did everything I knew to do, but God was in control of bringing him back, and He did.

Dustin's father explained that when he arrived at the hospital, they were bringing Wyatt in. He had no idea what to expect. He imagined the worst. Yet Wyatt was just sitting up on the gurney as if nothing had ever happened.

We stayed the night at the hospital as a precaution. The hospital bed was close to electrical outlets, for machines of course. Wyatt found them and kept trying to stick things in them. It made me so nervous I asked them if they could move the bed. What a little booger!

Once we settled in our room, that was when all the questioning began. It was horrible, devastating, and very uncomfortable. I felt treated like a criminal—not by authorities, but by a nurse who kept being so rude. I looked around the room at everybody, still in shock. The image of my baby lifeless replayed in my mind over and over.

I do understand why they have to ask questions, but the nurse's disapproving tone weighed on me. She kept repeating questions—*how did you do CPR? Show me exactly what you did. Where did you press? How hard?*

I'd just experienced the most devastating thing a mother would ever go through. Finding my child unconscious, incoherent, not breathing, and blue. Did I do something wrong by trying to save his life? Why were they treating me this way?

She went on, "Did you do CPR aggressively? The veins in his eyes are showing."

At one point I didn't even know what to say. What was she implying? The incident was all recorded with 911, and I barely had to do CPR. He came to rather quickly, by the grace of God.

Not one person in that room came to my defense. At that point, I knew something had to change. Another nurse entered and asked me if his veins always showed like that. I told her yes. As my only redhead, his skin was very pale. She was very nice and understanding.

I knew that God gave me Wyatt back. I know He was holding my hands during CPR. When I breathed in him, I believe He did also. It was all God, not me.

A doctor came into the room and told me a story about her little girl and a similar thing she experienced. The girl was riding her bike right by their fish pond and fell over, into the water. Had the doctor not been there, the child would have drowned. Accidents happen. They can happen when you are present and when you are not.

It grew late. Everyone started to leave, including my husband. I couldn't believe he didn't stay at the hospital with me that night. I looked around the room and realized I was all alone. Alone with my little Wyatt.

I'd never been in a position like this by myself. Many times throughout my life, I felt alone, but this was different. In Deuteronomy 31:8 it says it is the Lord who goes before you. He will be with you. He will not leave you or forsake you. Do not fear or be dismayed.

I know God was with me, but still, everything fell on my shoulders, the weight very heavy. Every decision, every problem, every answer, every responsibility, and even every outcome. I tried to control everything. I tried to do it all. At the time, I didn't realize that I didn't have to. Jesus can do all of these things for us if we will let Him.

As I sat there looking at my sweet Wyatt, thanking Jesus that he was alive, I started to cry. I wept with so much emotion. I remembered a time, right after Wyatt was born, when we played the part of Mary, Joseph, and baby Jesus in the church play. Wyatt, baby Jesus, was not even a month old. Watching him playing in that hospital bed brought such gratitude. Thank You, Jesus, for saving my baby.

I did not sleep that night at the hospital. The panic set in as the anxiety increased. Over and over I replayed the image of him so lifeless in my head. Panic attacks plagued me. For the first time in my life, I had to handle things all by myself. The nurses brought me crackers because I kept dry heaving from my nerves.

Something had to change. There had to be more to this life for me and my children than the life I was living. In the hospital that night, it was as if I grew up at the age of twenty-five and became a woman. A woman who was tired of living alone.

The next morning, I remember thinking I had no idea how to check him out of the hospital. I didn't remember where the parking deck was. I felt lost.

I hoped they would explain step by step what to do. By the grace of God, we checked out of the hospital, and I found the parking deck. As we were walking to my car, it felt so surreal. No doubt, I remained in a state of shock. I put Wyatt in the car and we drove home, just the two of us. I decided to go by the fire department, and thank everyone who came out that day and helped Wyatt. I also wanted them to see him and that he was okay.

As I headed home, I made my mind up. Things had to change. I needed to have a sit-down, real and serious, conversation with my husband. I went to him and asked if we could talk and we did. I expressed that I was lonely and that I needed more of his time, and that we needed to put God first in our marriage. I respected the fact that he was a hard worker who provided for his family. But I felt as though Dustin was away from us more than he should be. There was more that God had in store for us, and He would provide for all our needs. We just needed to obey Him.

CHAPTER 7

Life as a Single Mom

Two years went by with very little change. In fact, Dustin remained away from home even more. He spent more time with friends outside of work. Other things were taking place that I did not know of at the time, but I know now. We grew more distant, and the arguing, worse.

Dustin would fall asleep on the couch and never come to bed. I remember just lying there crying and longing for my husband to hold me, and to feel loved by him again. I asked myself how this happened. I even asked God why He had forsaken me and my marriage. I begged God to fix it. I prayed all the time. I didn't understand why my marriage was falling apart. Yet God allows us to make choices, and we cannot control what other people choose.

While Dustin turned to substance abuse, I found it very hard to turn away from the attention of other men. Something I previously had no problem with and always vehemently rejected the idea of. I always felt it was very disrespectful for someone to be flirtatious with me when they could clearly see I wore a wedding ring. What had changed in me to accept this kind of behavior? My answer was that I was lonely and not getting what I needed in my marriage. Still, I had a choice, and there isn't an excuse. I found myself praying again, begging God to fix my marriage, and confessing to Him how weak I was emotionally. I did not want my marriage to end. In fact, I said I would never divorce.

As things grew worse and worse, I knew the time had come. So many things happened that I could not get past. Boundaries crossed, trust broken. My marriage was sacred, and I honored my vows. How did this happen? How did things turn so ugly? How did the person I so dearly loved as my husband become someone I hardly even knew? I made the decision to see an attorney and file for a divorce.

I prayed about it a lot. There were grounds for divorce. We tried to work things out. We went to Christian counseling. I remember the counselor made me write everything down about a situation, and then she made me read it back to her out loud. Why did she make me relive such hurtful events? Dealing with this pain once was enough. I would leave there very angry and upset.

She would ask, after I finished reading out loud to her, "How does that make you feel"? The only answer that ever came to my mind—and truly how I felt—was *alone*. My answer was always alone. So alone.

I told the counselor after countless times and much prayer that I did not feel led to go back to or mend my marriage. I loved my husband, but I knew the relationship wasn't healthy. I wanted more for my children.

Things turned really ugly. Divorce isn't easy, and there is a reason that God hates it. We said so many hurtful things to one another. It was so painful. We bickered constantly, called the police on one another, and I would go to court broken and beaten down emotionally. I would leave there and ask myself, *what in the world just happened?* Why was this so hard? Would life ever get better?

The last time we went to court, a very wise judge gave us a piece of advice that I will never forget. He said, "You have marriage counseling to teach you how to be married before you get married, but there is no class that will ever teach you how to be divorced." He also said that if we continued to fight that our children would eventually blame themselves for the divorce.

From that moment on, I decided enough was enough. I love my children so much. I love them more than myself, and I would never want them to think they were to blame for any of this. From that point on, we made an effort to get along. It took baby steps. We realized we never really hated one another. We really loved one another, we just didn't know how to be apart.

I went through some really dysfunctional and abusive relationships throughout that time. Meanwhile, Dustin had another child. He protected me and our children in many ways, and I grew to love his girlfriend and newborn son. As hard as that was, I love my children so much, and sometimes, as a mother, we have to swallow our pride and do things for them that we normally would not do. I remember holding their little boy at a football game, thinking to myself what a sweet child he was. Often, my kids came home talking about him and how much fun he was to play with.

It definitely wasn't easy and even very hurtful at times. I would just tuck the pain away and be happy for their little hearts. A huge void developed in my life. I felt so alone, as if my family slowly slipped away. I couldn't offer my children what their father could financially.

I needed more time with them, but with working two jobs, how could I?

I worked five days a week doing skincare and styled hair on the side on the weekends. I was so stretched thin. I found myself crying out to God many times, praying. *There must be something more. I can't keep doing this. I need to be there for my kids.* Had I lost everything in the midst of trying to do the right thing and give them a better life?

Everything seemed to be working out great for their father. He went on to get his pilot license, bought an airplane, had a great job, and a new family. He used to warn me that no one would ever have me with three kids. That my package deal was just too much. Those lies sunk in. So I threw my own pity party. How could I ever be enough? Offer enough? Make enough? Find anyone who I would want to start another family with? Hopeless, loss, shame, and seclusion fell upon me like a dark cloud. Even though I would pray daily for God to help me, that huge void remained.

In 2010, I met someone at a very vulnerable and lonely point in my life. He said all the right things, and I believed every word of it. A polite and charming man, he even said he prayed for God to send him someone like me. I believed everything he said. Things moved very quickly in the relationship. We wanted the same things in life, right? This man and his words completely enamored me.

Words are so powerful. The Bible says in Proverbs 18: 20-21, *From the fruit of their mouth a person's stomach is filled; with the harvest of their lips they are satisfied. The tongue has the power of life and death, and those who love it will eat its fruit.* In this relationship, we both spoke of wanting to remarry and have a family again one day. We spoke of having more children.

Since things between us moved so quickly, I became pregnant right away. We started what I thought would be our life together.

CHAPTER 8

From Bliss to Broken...

This pregnancy was unlike any of the others. Then again, none of them were the same, as pregnancies go. We did find out what we were having early on—another sweet little girl. Brooke wanted me to have a girl, and the boys, well…I don't think they really cared. Nothing could damper my excitement.

We did have a little scare when the genetic screening came back abnormal. Scary at first, but we decided to do no further testing because we would love her no matter what. She would be perfect for us. It made me think of the verse in Genesis 1:27: *So God created mankind in his own image, in the image of God he created them; male and female he created them.* We knew that she was created in His perfect image, for a reason, and having purpose.

The relationship seemed great at first. As time went on, things started becoming more difficult. We were not married, and I became very confused about where my life was headed. This pregnancy, I found myself very emotional. My dad was so excited about me having another little girl. He said often that he could not wait to meet her.

As the relationship started growing distant, we began to see how different we really were. Honestly, I don't think he was ready for all of the responsibility. I think we have all wanted things in the moment, but when we get them, sometimes we realize it was more than we could handle.

My father also battled some things at this time. He had shoulder surgery, and his back was really giving him issues. They sent him to a pain clinic, where they prescribed him pain medicine. This medication made him hallucinate, and he became very troubled. He grew very paranoid and just plain miserable. At the time, I didn't realize how much it had taken over his mind.

One weekend my mom called and informed me she needed to take my dad to get some help to get off the medication. After they returned home, she explained that the doctors told him there was nothing they could do, and that he would have to go back to the pain clinic because he was not abusing the medication. I believe this news crushed my dad, and he became convinced there was no hope. The very next weekend, we had just finished eating dinner when there was a knock at our door. It was a police officer.

I thought, what in the world?

He said, "Are you Alison Butler?"

I replied, "Yes, I am."

He could see how pregnant I was. He said, "You might want to sit down."

"Okay…"

"I've come to let you know that your father has taken his life."

He explained that they were doing an investigation at my mom's house. I asked if I could go to her, but the answer was a harsh but compassionate no. I needed to wait until they finished things up.

I hit my knees in the hallway, sobbing. How could my daddy be gone? Things grew even harder in my relationship after that. In my heart, I knew that it was not going to last.

I gave birth to my sweet little girl in February of 2011. We named her Payton Leigh. My middle name is Leigh and so was my father's. Although I was out of the will of God with my actions, Payton was in the will of God. What a precious gift she is. The Bible says in Psalms 127:3: *Children are a heritage from the Lord, offspring a reward from him.*

As time went on, the relationship came to an end. If I could describe how this relationship affected me, it would be that I felt like a used piece of trash. Just wadded up and thrown away like it never even existed.

After my first marriage, I'd told myself if there ever was a time that I was raising my boys to be better men than the man that I was with, it was time to move on from that relationship.

I'd tried doing things my way instead of God's way, which ended on a road of destruction again. I moved in with my mother until I could get my feet on the ground. Payton was only four months old. Payton's father and I remained civil and somewhat of friends.

I think we were both very confused. It was very hard for me. I remember seeing what my other children went through with my divorce. I didn't want another one to have a broken home. As time went by and seasons rolled on, we continued to try to see each other. Like most relationships, we tried one more go-around. As we all know, most of the time things don't change. I carried a lot of hope that it would though.

CHAPTER 9

Jesus Carried Me

Things were going really well. Christmas 2011 approached, and I remember being really happy. Brooke and I made a lot of Christmas candy that year. I was able to get them everything they asked for. I even had a surprise ski trip planned, with ski clothing under the tree.

Brooke was a high school basketball cheerleader. I remember going and watching her cheer, attending Christmas parties at school, and doing all the fun things families do before Christmas. It was about to be Christmas break. My children were healthy and life was good.

That Christmas, Brooke asked if she could go with her dad to take her uncle home to Texas. That is where he lived, and she wanted to go see her cousins. I told her if that was what she wanted, I didn't mind. Dustin, her father, would fly them home after they'd visited here in Georgia.

They planned to head out on that Monday, December 19 and would return that Thursday, December 22. Just in time for Christmas. I would have her home to spend the holiday with her. As the days led up to their departure, we did some Christmas shopping together, and also enjoyed watching movies and spending time together, as we usually did on the weekend.

That Sunday, the night before she left, I remember asking her to come downstairs and spend some time with me. She called back, "I am packing, Mom." So, of course, I went to her. I have always lived as though nothing is guaranteed in this life. That anything can happen at any given time. So my words to her were this: "Baby, I just want to spend some time with you before you go." So we talked as she packed, and then we went to bed. On the morning of December 19, the day they were leaving to take Dustin's brother home, it was beautiful outside. The sun shined so pretty. I remember sitting at the computer, looking up some things. I always wanted to run in the Peachtree Road Race here where we live, so I was checking out when I could register for that.

Brooke sat down with me, and I explained what I was doing. She said, "Well, Momma, I'll run in that race with you if you want me to, but I probably won't be able to run the entire race. We might have to walk some of it."

I said, "Baby, there is no way I could run that entire race. But I would love for us to do that."

We both laughed. "It'll be so much fun!

For some reason, I was very emotional that day. We were sitting there and I just looked at her and said, "Brooke, you know I am your parent, and I love you so much. I protect you and I guide you, but you are my best friend."

She replied, "I know, Momma. You tell me everything."

Tears began to fill up in my eyes and again I said, "I love you so much."

She said, "I love you, too." Then she asked, "What's wrong? Why are you crying?"

I said, "Oh, I don't know, probably just having an emotional day like us women do."

We hugged and laughed some more. Dustin got a late start and was running behind schedule. I remember telling her bye and to call me every chance that she could. She made jokes about not getting a good signal and standing on a hay bale, holding her phone in the sky in order to find one. She'd just received an early Christmas present, which happened to be a new iPhone.

So off they went. The rest of us had a busy day planned too. We had Christmas shopping to finish! The other kids and I dressed and started our day, which turned out very different in so many ways, now that I look back on it. We shopped until we dropped. We went from store to store—and I don't mean in a mall, I mean all over the place. I have always been about a good sale, so whatever it takes, right?

That afternoon, I spoke with Brooke on the phone. They'd stopped in Mississippi to fuel up and eat some lunch. She shared that she just couldn't rest on this flight. I asked her what was wrong, but she replied, "I don't know." I asked her about some Christmas presents she'd wanted and encouraged her to eat some lunch and try to rest. I reminded her that I loved her and to text me as soon as they landed.

Again, something about that day stands out as very different. I just couldn't stop for some reason. I stayed very busy. That evening, when we finally finished shopping and were on our way home, I said to the boys and Payton, "Let's rent a movie and go home and relax."

One of the boys replied, "Mom, I feel like we've been on a trip. We have been gone all day and been so busy."

I agreed, "I am tired."

So we returned home, unloaded the car, and prepared for bed and our movie. We all got comfy and started a film about a girl who returns from college with dreams of being a writer.

Meanwhile, Brooke texted and explained they were taking a different route due to some storms, and it would take a little longer to arrive. I texted her back, telling her once again that I loved her and to text me as soon as they landed. By the end of the movie, my mom, Jacob, and Payton had all fallen asleep. Wyatt and I were the night owls, so we were still awake.

I thought to myself, let me call Brooke. I hadn't heard from her and it seemed to be taking longer than I expected for them to land. I texted, asking if they were there yet. She replied back, *No, we are still in the plane and it is storming.*

How much longer do you have before you get there? I asked.

No reply, which is very common in a plane since your signal can go in and out.

Just text me when you land! Love you!

Time went by. Still no reply. Surely they had landed by now. I called Brooke. No answer. But she was probably at the airport, waiting on Dustin's brother's wife to pick them up. Either she just couldn't get to her phone, or she didn't have a signal.

I sat down at my computer, feeling really anxious. I decided to track the plane. I'd never done that before, and I had no idea how. I knew I needed the tail number. I turned on the computer and of all times, the DSL went out. I slammed my fist down on the desk, feeling very frustrated. My son, Wyatt, came in and said, "Mom, what's wrong?"

"I need to track the plane, and the computer isn't working. Who could help us do that?"

I immediately called Dustin's mom. "Have you heard from Dustin? Have they landed?"

She explained that his brother's wife had tracked the plane. They were thirty minutes from landing, and she was headed to the airport to pick them up.

"Oh…okay…can you call me if you hear from them?"

I hung the phone up. Why did I feel so anxious? I sat there in silence for a moment and then all of a sudden the craziest thing happened.

I felt heat crawl up my spine to my neck, then to the back of my head. The sensation wrapped around to my forehead. Then it felt as if someone stood on my chest and ripped my soul out.

I gasped for air, trying to take a deep breath, and started crying hysterically. I rushed into my mother's room and woke her up crying.

"What's wrong? What is it?"

All I could say was, "I need Brooke back on a commercial plane right now." I kept repeating it over and over again. "I need Brooke back on a commercial plane now."

I grabbed my phone and called Melissa again for an update. Dustin's brother's wife was now at the airport and in communication with her dad.

"If you want," she suggested, "you and Wyatt can come over here."

Wyatt and I jumped in the car and headed that way. When we arrived, I learned Melissa contacted some friends and they were on their way over.

I sat on the couch, my leg jumping up and down. A sense of dread and doom settled over me like a black cloud. I couldn't stand it. I wanted to run. To scream. There was no denying it now. At any moment, someone would approach and tell me the bad news. News I had already had to hear the previous year about my dad.

My leg kept shaking, moving nonstop. Up and down, up and down. My skin crawled. I could burst from waiting. I had to do something, so I told Melissa that I was going to go wake up Payton's father and to call me if she heard anything.

The entire ride to his house, only ten minutes away, I just kept calling all of them. Brooke. Dustin. His wife. I kept begging in my head, over and over, *please text me Brooke, please call, please, please, please call me.* I would get voicemail, hang up, and dial again. Brooke. Dustin. His wife. No answer.

One last time. But all of their phones were dead; they all went straight to voicemail. When I arrived at Payton's father's house, I banged on the door and managed to wake him. It was getting late by this time. I explained that I didn't know what was going on but that I had not heard back from Brooke. He could see the panic, the anxiety, and the agony on my face. He could hear it in my voice.

My phone rang—Dustin's mom. When I picked up, she asked, "Is Payton's dad there?"

"Yes."

"Could you hand him the phone?"

Shock vibrated through me as I slowly handed him the phone. He repeated every word that she said. "Dustin's brother's wife's dad got in touch with the state patrol who got in touch with the NTSB, and they located the plane."

The next statement out of his mouth I will never forget. How his words felt or the look on my little Wyatt's face. The smell in the air. I remember it so vividly. "They've found the plane. There's been an accident, and there are no survivors."

CHAPTER 10

I Will Never Let Her Go

My world crumbled. I went into shock. My body completely shut down, and I dropped to my knees. I belted out a scream. The word "NO!" shredded the air around me until I broke down. I will never forget Wyatt's little voice or the moment that he did the same. He yelled, "NO" and held the cry until he broke. Broken-hearted. Broken tears. Broken children. Broken everything. That moment completely tore apart my world.

I went into survival mode.

The pain, the grief, is not something you can imagine. I can't explain what your body and your mind does or how it manages except for Jesus and His grace. I grabbed my phone, not really knowing what I was doing or saying. I just kept repeating, "No, no, no, no," over and over again. I begged God to please give her back. I pleaded with Him. I cried out, "You are a God of miracles! Please just give her back! Please don't take her! Please, please, please I am begging you!"

I called my closest friend, who I'd known since we were five years old. "She's gone, she's gone, she's gone…"

She started asking frantic questions.

"My best friend is gone…she's gone. They all went, the plane crashed, they are all gone…."

Somehow I pulled myself together enough to ask Payton's dad to drive us. We headed back to my mom's still in utter incredulity. I remembered looking at Wyatt—so quiet and in shock—wondering what we were going to do. When I explained to my mom, she was in total disbelief. She even called Dustin's mom, saying, "Please tell me this isn't true."

I needed to wake Jacob, my other son, to tell him the news. Bless his heart, the first thing out of his mouth was, "Is Brooke okay?"

I answered, "No, son, she is not. They have all gone to be with Jesus."

As a mother, trying to process that I had just lost my daughter was incredibly hard much less to be a comfort to anyone else at that time. Having to look at my two sons and witness their pain of losing a father, a sister, a brother, a stepmom, and an uncle… I just can't even begin to tell you how ugly and overwhelming that feels. How lost I was.

In a state of shock, I went into a fog, as if in a dream, a terrible nightmare. Yet my body kicked into survival mode and kept going, kept doing the things I needed it to.

I'd stayed up all night, and suddenly I just had to lay down. The emotion overwhelming me was terrible. All the tears, the groans, the heartache, and the agony. Almost unbearable. The darkness, all the whys.

How do I go on like this? constantly played over and over in my head as the days went on. Sleep felt impossible, and yet, my body demanded it.

My life was changed in an instance and changed forever. I would just look around in a daze—at the Christmas tree and all of her presents. At my children. Not being able to help them or heal their pain overwhelmed me. All the wonderful people who came to visit. I couldn't even tell you who was there because mentally I was not. I would wake every morning and lay on the bathroom floor and dry heave. The reality would hit me that it was not a dream. I would cry until it just completely wore me out. No appetite, no sleep, just existing in a daze.

My mom came to me and said that the funeral home had called. They wanted to come out and talk about the arrangements. I remember all of us sitting around the dining room table. All that kept running through my mind was that I needed my baby back. How soon could we get her back? Where was she? Where did they take her?

The accident happened in Texas, so I had no idea about the process and not one—not even one—investigator called me about my child. They may have spoken to someone else, but they did not speak to me directly, and no one told me if they did. I was in no shape to talk anyway. I do know people had my phone. They would not let me turn on the TV. The crash was national, so it was all over the news. They loved me and were just trying to protect me from more pain.

While we were sitting at the table going over some of the funeral options, through my fog I heard, "No one is viewable. I would not suggest anyone see or view them." I looked up and hysterically started crying. My body rocked back and forth in the chair. What did my precious Brooke go through?

"Please, God," I cried out loud. "I have to hold her one more time." I had to get her back. I had to get my baby back!

The funeral directors looked at my mom and suggested I might need to take something for my nerves. What good would that do? It wouldn't take the pain away. It wouldn't bring my daughter back. I was already dazed enough…why would I want to be in a fog even more?

After hearing that, I decided that I was going to be of sound mind. No one was going to tell me that I couldn't see her, hold her, and kiss her sweet face one more time.

A friend finally explained to me that the accident had made national headlines. A news crew had even been to my house, and I had no idea.

One night, I decided to look up the articles on my phone. What I read took my breath away again. It stated that my daughter Brooke had been ejected from the plane. The wing on the side of the plane where she was sitting had been ripped off. She was the only one who was ejected. There was no fire, just a mangled-up piece of steel. I saw the pictures of the plane, and it all started to become very real.

I began to wonder and ask myself, *What did my baby go through? Was it instant? Was it terrible? Was she scared? Did she know? Did she suffer long? Did she want her mom? Did she feel alone?* I wasn't there to hold her hand. I wasn't there to protect her. I wasn't there to tell her it would be okay. She must have been terrified. God why, why did this have to happen? I screamed out... "WHY?!"

Then he spoke to my heart clearly. *I never promised you a day with her. She was a gift and I gave you almost fifteen years.* I began to think differently. I was blessed. I was blessed that He chose me to be her mom for fourteen years. Even if it were just a day, I was chosen and I was blessed.

I remember reading a book a couple of months before the crash. One thing that stuck out to me in the book was about a little girl who passed. God said, "She was strong. I never left her." I felt like that was exactly how it was for Brooke.

I know without a shadow of a doubt that Jesus was there. I know that He never left Brooke. I believe He was there holding her hand. I believe that He took her out of the plane and placed her exactly where they found her. I also believe that He did that for me. I believe He would say to her, "This is for your mom, who loves you so much and is going to hold you one last time."

The verse 2 Corinthians 5:8 occurred to me often. *We are confident, I say, and willing rather to be absent from the body, and to be present with the Lord.*

To be absent from the body—meaning death—is to be present with the Lord—meaning Life. As soon as she took her last breath, she was in the presence of Jesus.

CHAPTER 11

God's Mercy

I did not sleep that entire week. Waiting patiently to get my daughter's body back home was torture. I sat out on my mom's porch at night, sometimes in the freezing rain, just rocking and staring at the trees. I always had a friend with me. We smoked a lot of cigarettes, a bad habit I would turn to if I was stressed or something happened in my life. I guess that was my "go-to." I never got caught up in drugs, and I wasn't a big drinker. Smoking just seemed to calm my nerves.

One night, God gave me a vision. The plane appeared just as it had on the news. Cold rain drizzled in the night, and Brooke stood away from the plane, the others strewn in the distance. She was just standing there, Jesus bent down on one knee in front of her, almost as if someone were going to propose. He held her hands in His. The love that she felt I can't explain, but I know it was unlike anything she'd ever experienced before. She was not afraid.

In my vision, she said to Him, "My mom needs me. I need to go to her."

Jesus replied with this, "I need your mom to stay because I am not done with her, but you will be with her again very soon."

She said, "Okay." Jesus stood, and the group all came together and walked away holding hands.

Brooke was saved at the young age of six, so she knew of Jesus and learned about Him in church. I believe that it did not feel strange to her—that it all made perfect sense to her. As the week went on—the longest week of my life—I received a phone call from a sweet lady from the funeral home (who also later became a dear friend of mine).

She told me, "Alison, we think Brooke can be viewed." The funeral home in Texas in current possession of her had shared this information. In my mind, I was so thankful, although I would have seen her, held her, and kissed her sweet face one last time no matter what.

That was a Friday night, and they explained that they were sending Brooke and Dustin back on a plane together. Even though I knew they were no longer with us, it was comforting to know that she was not alone. I ached so badly to have them home. Such thoughts seemed surreal. At times, I still questioned if this was even happening.

Later that night, I received a phone call from the same dear lady at the funeral home that she had picked Dustin and Brooke up at the airport. They'd arrived at the funeral home. She explained, "Alison, you can see Brooke, but I do not suggest anyone viewing Dustin."

The day came that I got to hold my sweet little girl. That week had been horrible. Picking out a casket, finding pictures and music, a nightmare in itself. Making an obituary and a funeral program, misery. Asking people she cared about to speak at the funeral, overwhelming. Picking out what she would wear, gut-wrenching. I could not have done it without my mom and my sister and my friends. Every day went by in an ugly blur and felt like a daze. As if I wasn't even there.

I remember choosing the pearl white casket and saying, "That one—she would want that one." Her favorite flowers were yellow roses. I decided she'd be buried in her cheerleading uniform. It was so much. God literally had to carry me through this process.

The community came together and honored Brooke in so many ways. Her teachers, friends, classmates, cheerleaders, the football players and so on. People posted candles outside their homes, lit in memory of her. Candlelight vigils and an outpouring of support from churches and people ensured we always had a hot meal every single night for weeks. Even though I existed in a thick fog, not fully present in my mind, I will never forget the love the community provided us.

Christmas Eve, a Saturday, was the day I got to see and hold my Brooke one last time.

I was nervous and fearful. What would I see? What would it be like? How I wanted to hold her, feel her, clinch her hand, kiss her face, and tell her how much I loved her.

I only allowed a few people to see her. When I arrived at the funeral home, they explained that they only had to fix a few things, one being her chin. They had to build it up because apparently she took a hard hit there. After they explained, we walked to the room. My heart was beating and pounding so fast but also breaking at the same time. I had to take a deep breath when they opened the door. I walked in slowly, very slowly, and I was in disbelief at what I saw.

As I slowly walked over, observing her broken body lying on what looked like a stretcher, I put my hands on her face, kissed her lips, rubbed her beautiful brown hair and told her how sorry I was that I was not there. That I could not get to her and that it took so long to get her back. I just kept saying, "I am so sorry. I love you so, so much."

As I looked at her face, I thought to myself, *What happened? What happened? How did my baby die?* Her face appeared almost perfect, just a couple of scratches, no bruising, and no swelling. Her soft hair shined just like always. One might think her asleep. But as I began to touch her arm and her hand, I noticed just how broken she was. Her wrist was broken, her body shifted. Her rib cage was lifted on one side and her hip broken. Her feet dangled because both of her ankles were broken. The most damage seemed to be on her left side—the side that came out of the plane first from where she was sitting. Her body had shifted because of the force, and I would assume the suction of coming out of the plane. When the wing came off, it left a hole right where she sat. She took a very hard hit above her knees and had what looked like road rash, likely from the seat belt trying to hold her body in, but the force was just too powerful.

But her face…her sweet face was just perfect. She must have hit her chin at some time but other than that she looked like my sweet Brookie. I sat there beside her, just staring at her in disbelief. I didn't want to leave. They told me to take all the time I needed, and I did. I knew I had to accept that she was gone. I needed to see her to accept that. I understood she was with Jesus and began to get some strength and comfort knowing where she was. The hardest part was leaving her.

I asked if I could see her again before the funeral. They said it would not be a good idea, as they were not able to embalm any of them. Their veins and bodies were just too damaged. They proceeded to explain that with time, her body would change, and she would not look the same. I acknowledged that I understood, still disappointed. I gave them her cheerleading uniform, and I went back to her again. I held her one last time, kissed her again, and told her how much I loved her and how much I was going to miss her. As I started to leave, I said, "You little booger. You got to go before me and meet Jesus, and I am a little jealous. I will be with you one day. When it is my time to meet Jesus. There is no time in heaven like here on earth, so it won't be long. For me, it will feel like a lifetime here on earth. I love you, and I will carry you in my heart until we meet again." Then I left the room.

I asked the sweet lady at the funeral home, "Isn't it just crazy how people can break every bone in their body and survive? Her face looks perfect. You did a wonderful job getting her ready for me. Her part in her hair was perfect, and thank you for not putting makeup on her. She didn't really wear much makeup at the age of fourteen."

I asked more questions later because I just kept wondering about so many things. Had her neck been broken?

"No, no, Alison," my friend explained. "It was not and there was no way she ever landed on her face. Her eyes were not black, and her face was not swollen."

Even she seemed a little confused about Brooke's injuries, all from her chest down, her face intact.

I understood it was God. He had mercy on me, knowing I would see her no matter what. I know He took her out of that plane and placed her in a field for me. And I knew I had to let her go.

CHAPTER 12

Christmas Eve

When we left the funeral home, we went on to the cemetery to pick out grave plots and discuss vaults and headstones. Such surreal conversations. It rained every day that week. Dustin needed to be put in two grave plots because the ground was so soft, and with four of them being buried beside one another, the groundskeepers were afraid the soil would cave.

The people who work such jobs are heaven-sent. The kind woman I met at the cemetery was amazing. Her job couldn't be easy, but she went above and beyond to make sure everything was perfect, to ease burdens, and make decisions.

I don't know what I would have done without my family and friends that day. They all were so willing to help and accompanied me everywhere. They never left my side.

We returned home, and I started looking for more pictures to use. I still needed to decide on all the pallbearers. So many had volunteered, every one of them so sweet and without hesitation honored to do this for my sweet Brooke. But when my boys requested to carry their sister, it just broke my heart. Of course, I said yes. She wouldn't want it any other way.

That evening, Christmas Eve, things started to settle down. As tradition, we would always open presents with my parents and sister on that day. They handed me all of Brooke's presents to open for her. I always buy everyone matching PJs, and we open them and wear them on Christmas Eve. As I was sitting there opening these presents, one by one the tears just started flowing uncontrollably. My heart ached so badly. How could I ever not be broken again? I would never spend another Christmas with my Brookie.

I can't even explain this most horrible pain. Every bit of my body hurt. Just agonizing, awful torture. I tried to pull it together, but I just couldn't. I sobbed.

"I left her there. She is laying in that funeral home, and she looks so beautiful, and I am not there with her."

My mind frequently traveled back and forth to what I call "the flesh," which could not understand, and my spiritual side, which knew exactly where she was—and that she would never want to come back. That night, my mother came to me and told me something that changed everything.

Earlier that week, the pastor came to visit and talk with the family. I don't really remember much about him being there, but I do remember him telling me something that my son Jacob said. He was only eleven years old at the time. He said, "This is life and a part of life and we must go on." I couldn't believe those were the words of an eleven-year-old boy, my son. Yes, this was a part of life and unfortunately, a part of life that some of us have to go through.

That night, Christmas Eve, Wyatt, my younger son, decided that he was going to wear Brooke's PJs that I'd bought her for Christmas. They were pink of all colors. Wyatt and Brooke were very close and just a few weeks before he spent his birthday money on her and bought her a poster. He would do anything she said. He looked up to her as the oldest sibling.

Before we went to bed, my mom came to me and explained that Jacob had come to her and asked her if we could put Brooke's remaining presents somewhere else rather than open them on Christmas morning. She asked him why, and he told her that he just couldn't stand to see his mom like this anymore. He said the pain was too much, watching me like this. He didn't want to see me cry anymore.

I realized that I had to get it together. My kids needed me. They'd lost so much.

Children watch how we deal with situations. We mold them and help create who they will become as adults one day.

At that point, I knew my grief needed to be put aside for the time being, for the sake of my children. As mothers, we love our children more than we love ourselves. So there are many times in life you must put your emotions aside for them.

We were getting closer to the day of the funeral, to take place on Tuesday, December 27. We went about getting our clothes together, suits and ties for the boys, haircuts, and new shoes. It was so dreary and rainy. That week seemed like a lifetime.

That weekend, I had a dream. In it, the phone rang. I answered and said, Hello."

Dustin's voice came across the line, clear as day. He said, "Hey."

I said, "Hey," and then I paused and added, "Is it true?"

"What is true?"

"Absent from the body, present with the Lord."

He answered, "Yes, it's true."

"Did you all go together?"

"Yes, we all went at the same time."

Then the phone hung up.

That next morning, I called a friend of mine and described the dream. "Why didn't I ask about Brooke? Why didn't I ask what she was doing?"

She replied, "What you asked answered every question you could ever have."

"You're right. All that matters is knowing where they are. There is no greater place to be."

CHAPTER 13

When I Heard Her Voice

On the day before the funeral, I sat in the bathtub in a daze, as I'd been all week, when something happened. I heard her voice…her sweet little voice. I could hear her so clearly. She sounded so excited and joyful and so happy. "Momma, Momma, Momma! You have got to tell them! You have got to tell them where I am, and how to get here, please! You have to tell them."

"Okay, I will," I agreed—and I knew at that very moment I would not leave that church until I told everyone where my sweet Brookie was.

I informed the pastor I needed to add one more person to speak...myself. I didn't know how I was going to do it, or if I could even speak clearly enough for people to understand me. I asked myself over and over, *Can I hold back the tears long enough to say it? Can I get through this?* But I had to. God would carry me through it, as he had all week long. God would speak through me.

We headed to the funeral home that morning for all the families to meet so we could follow one another to the church. I asked myself again, *Is this really happening? Is this a nightmare? Am I just in a really bad dream?*

We arrived, and all the caskets were loaded in the hearses. Our cars lined up, then we prayed before we headed to the church.

This is the day I would bury my daughter.

When we arrived at the church, the staff waited there for us and escorted us to a room off to the side. The choir room, perhaps. I had no idea what was going on, but I could see there were a lot of people present. The chapel was full. People crowded into overflow rooms.

I think I went into shock as we entered the chapel. My eyes could only focus on the white casket and the beautiful picture of Brooke in her cheerleading uniform placed by it on a stand. The yellow roses on the casket—so pretty. All the people turned into a blur.

The music played, the preacher spoke, and the videos of Brooke played. Then it was time for people to speak. They called everyone's name: her friends, teachers, my friends, cheerleading coaches…but not mine. *But I have something to say! I promised her I would say it, and I have to say it!* I looked at one of the pastors and mouthed the words, "I need to say something." He returned in the same manner, "You want to say something?" Then all of a sudden, he called my name. I walked up on the stage with two of Brooke's best friends by my side.

I really can't remember what all I said, but I do remember this. I said, "What would Brookie say to you all right now? What would she want you to know? It would be that this place is unimaginable, it is amazing, awesome, holy, joyful, full of love, and no pain. She would want you to know how to get there. She wants to see you all again.

"Brooke was saved at the young age of six, at a Vacation Bible School. Because Brooke knew Jesus as her Lord and Savior and asked Him to come into her heart and believed that He died on the cross for her sins, He gave her the everlasting gift, the greatest gift of all and that is eternal life.

"A life after death. A life that is more alive than we are living here on earth. More alive than she could ever describe to us. One that we will never experience until we get there." I looked at all of the young people—her schoolmates, the cheerleaders, the football players, the basketball players—and reminded them that Brooke would want to see each and every one of them again.

If you declare with your mouth, "Jesus is Lord," and believe in your heart that God raised him from the dead, you will be saved. Romans 10:9

For, everyone who calls on the name of the Lord will be saved. Romans 10:13

I remember looking at the parents and saying this one word that I know God laid on my heart and was speaking through me. The word was "listen." "Listen to your children and I mean listen. Life can get so busy, and sometimes we may not hear what they are trying to tell us, because we are so caught up in our own lives. Listen, they need that, they need to be heard."

As the funeral ended, there was one last song to be played—one of my favorites. It is "How Great Thou Art." The lady who sang it did a beautiful job. I will forever hold a place for her in my heart. As I sat there looking at the white casket, the picture, and the yellow roses, in such a fog, that song—that beautiful song—just moved me. I could have sat there for days just listening to it. I didn't want it to end.

Each of the football players and cheerleaders made their way to the casket to place a yellow rose. As they walked by me, they hugged my neck in a display of the love they had for my daughter.

At that point, suddenly the music sounded different, as if I could really hear. Does that make sense? I can't say I've ever heard anything like it, as if I could hear every note, as if I could feel it. I appreciated it in a way I never had a song before. I recalled watching Dustin play the guitar, and the way he could hear the music as I didn't.

So while I listened to the words in the song "How Great Thou Art," some people might say there was nothing great about this. What good could come from this? But the great thing is not the loss, obviously—it's the way God carries us through the loss.

He is a faithful father. One who saves us, carries us, takes us by the hand, and leads us. He holds us at night while we cry so hard that our bodies and our minds physically and emotionally just give out and are completely drained. He gives us rest when we need it. He never leaves us. He sits with us day in and day out. He lives within us and He is awesome. Those are the great things.

It is not that God is good because I have lost a child, and now I have to live the rest of my life without her. It is this: God is good because now I will depend on Him the rest of my life to get up, to keep going, and to be the mother to my other children that He has blessed me with. Without God, I could not live the rest of my life without her. He is my lifeline. He is how I survive.

When it was time to walk out of the auditorium, everyone filed out in a line, and proceeded outside. I found myself standing alone, wondering yet again if this could be a bad dream.

There were three hearses, three caskets, Brooke's carried by her brothers and friends. They were loaded, and the burial followed. I looked around, feeling lost. I saw one of Brooke's friends, who I walked over to. The moment was so surreal. Everyone began finding their cars and lining up to go to the cemetery.

When we arrived at the cemetery, the tents stood and chairs lined the area. The hearses stopped to unload. It was time. Time to bury my baby and say my final goodbye to this part of the journey. The last final step of this process.

Still in a fog, I exited my car and stepped on soft, muddy ground from all the rain that week. I stood there in a daze, watching the events unfolding around me as in a nightmare.

Dustin's friends and family carried him, his son, and his wife. Then there was Brooke. My boys, my friends, my friend's husbands carried her to her resting place. I followed behind, still in disbelief. The burial seemed quick and just for a second the sun peaked out. When they dismissed us, I stood and looked at that white pearl casket covered with beautiful yellow roses. I placed my hands on it and took a deep breath. My heart hurt, my chest felt so heavy. As I placed my hands on the casket and stared at it, so many things ran through my mind. I just leaned down and kissed the top of that white pearl casket one last time. One last kiss for my baby girl.

At that moment, I understood only her flesh was going in the ground. Her sweet little spirit flew high in heaven. A new chapter of this awful nightmare would now begin—having to learn to live without her.

It began to rain, but the light was coming. It had to. It had been dark for so long. It could not end here. There were miracles to come.

Although I've made many mistakes throughout my life and felt alone a lot of the time, I can see looking back how Jesus was always there, and it was all a part of the process of bringing me closer to Him. If I had not made my mistakes, caused by my poor decisions and frequent screw-ups, I would never have seen Jesus the way I do or felt the need to rely on Him.

For some of us. The road traveled in life is more difficult. But I am here to tell you, God can save you. I am living proof. For those who think they have lived the perfect life, there is no such thing.

In Romans 3:23 the Bible says: *For we all have sinned and fallen short of the glory of God, and All are justified freely by his grace through the redemption that came by Jesus Christ.*

To say you have not sinned is to take pride in one's self, which is sin.

I used to hang my head in shame for my wrongdoings, but I don't have to do that anymore. I have been set free. Free from those chains of shame. Free from guilt. Free from all the poor decisions. That is why Jesus died for us. He wanted to set us free from all of our sins. He wanted to save us. He gave us everlasting life.

I had to quit believing the enemies' lies about me. I had to rise up and know my self-worth. I had to hold my head high and remember who my father is. He is the King of all Kings and Lord of all Lords. He is the Prince of Peace.

In John Chapter 8, the Bible talks about a woman who was caught in adultery. Jesus said, "Let anyone among you who is without sin be the first to throw a stone at her."

We all have sinned in some way, and those sins can be washed. We all can be sanctified and justified in the name of the Lord Jesus Christ and by the Spirit of our Living God.

In my the next part of this book, *Bringing Light to the Loss*, I will tell you how much my life changed when I decided to do things God's way and not my own. I hope you will continue to come on this journey with me, and I pray you will find freedom in Jesus.

He gives power to the weak, and to those who have no might he increases strength. Even youths shall faint and be weary, and the young men shall fall, but those who wait on the Lord shall renew their strength; they shall mount up with wings like eagles, they shall run and not be weary, they shall walk and not faint. Isaiah 40:29-30

Bringing Light

to the Loss

Living Life with an Empty Void

CHAPTER 1

My Saving Grace

On December 27th, 2011 I buried my beautiful daughter. My firstborn. We also buried my first husband, and my boys' stepmother, and little brother.

After the burial, we returned home exhausted and not knowing where life would take us next. As a family, we would get up every day and just try to trudge through. Depression became a dark cloud. I would be so exhausted at night because it literally took all of my energy to manage.

When I woke in the morning, I remember often sitting up and placing my feet on the floor and saying to myself, "This is my life. It is not a dream." Then I would pray, asking God, *Please...please just help me get through this day.*

We all felt so lost and clung to each other for support and love.

I also had my sweet little baby Payton to take care of. She was so little at the time. My boys were ten and eleven years old. Eventually, they returned to school. Thankfully, the teachers and staff were so helpful in this time of sorrow. Going back to our everyday lives and routines proved incredibly difficult. Life was forever changed. It was as if the fog wouldn't lift.

One day, a friend called and suggested an idea that made perfect sense. In fact, it gave me chills, almost as if Brooke took part in it. My friend thought we should do a race in honor of Brooke, with the proceeds going to graduating seniors. She'd no idea that Brooke and I were planning to run in our first 5k ever right before she left.

I burst out, "I think that sounds like a great idea! It's perfect. Let's do it!" This was the start of the Brooke Butler Memorial Races that began in 2012 and continued until 2015, the year Brooke would have graduated high school. The first 5k race that I ever ran was in memory of my daughter.

The school continued to remember Brooke's memory as well. They would set her pom-poms out at basketball games in the place where she would have stood to cheer. They even placed a shadow box with her uniform in the gym.

A non-profit organization, Caring for a Cause, handled her memorial races and we had many themes. We held a color run, a superhero race, and a farewell race on the year she would have graduated. I will forever be grateful for my friend who started these races and to Caring for a Cause for making them happen. They were literally heaven-sent.

Although those days were so exhausting and so hard to get through, I loved seeing everyone come out and honor Brooke's memory. It meant so much. I thoroughly enjoyed seeing all the kids having fun and dressing up for the themes. All of my loved ones and friends and even strangers came out and supported these races. We had many sponsors that were so kind to give. She was so loved.

Brooke was an old soul. She loved so hard, and she was an amazing friend to many. She could light up a room, and her laughs were contagious. She was a great kid and a great role model to her brothers. Brooke cherished her family and never wanted to see anyone hurt. She enjoyed going to concerts, cheering, and dancing. Brooke was fearless! She worked hard in school, was an excellent student and never gave me any problems. I was so blessed to be chosen as her mother. To know her is to love her. I am grateful for the fourteen years with my sweet angel.

CHAPTER 2

Making a Move

One of the biggest milestones after Brooke's passing was our family moving into a new home—starting a new chapter, one that would never be the same. I couldn't stay at my mom's forever and of course, we needed more room. About eight months passed, and I began to look for a house for me and my children. It was time. Time for a move.

Previously, I'd bought some land that I had planned to build a house on one day. I always wanted a mountain-style home with a lot of windows and wood, from the floor to the ceiling.

One Sunday afternoon, I started looking online for homes for sale. I thought to myself how great it would be if I found a house like I always wanted in our school district.

Lo and behold, it happened. The house I'd always dreamed of was put on the market that weekend, and it was in our school district. It was just like what I wanted to build on our land. I know it was from God. I believe Brooke had her hand in it as well.

I began the process of purchasing the home, and we moved in that August, right before school started. We loved this place, but it still felt so unreal. It was the first home I'd purchased on my own, but it was also the first one that I'd never decorated or set up a room for Brooke in. I felt so lost in so many ways.

Often, the three kids and I would all just pile up and sleep in my room. Sometimes we wouldn't even eat in the kitchen. We'd just escape to my room and eat. I remember asking the boys if they felt as if someone just dropped us off at this house and said, "Here you go…now live." They both answered yes. We had a beautiful new home, but we were all still walking around in survival mode, just existing, still in shock.

When we separated, Dustin bought a truck. At that time, I was in a weird stage of almost divorced. A time when you are trying to figure out the decisions you've made, while that person had been all you knew for twelve years and no matter how angry or done you are, you also tend to want to be around them. Maybe in hopes of working things out at times, but also because you miss them and tend to forget all of the hurtful things that have happened. Especially when you are lonely. We went out on a date in that truck. I remember him taking me out to eat and us just riding around, talking.

My oldest son, Jacob, came to me and said, "I want Daddy's truck."

I said, "Okay, son, I will do whatever I have to. We will keep it up and running just for you." About a week later, the truck was brought to our home. After it was parked, when I was alone, I would look out the window at it in the driveway and just cry. Once, I walked out to the truck, put my hand on the door handle, and just wept. I almost fell to my knees sobbing.

I opened the door, climbed in the seat, placed my hands on the steering wheel, and just bawled my eyes out. I touched anything and everything that he would have touched. I laid my head on the steering wheel and just cried out, "Why, why did you leave us? Why did you have to go? Our boys need you." I was so scared of raising them alone. At that moment I made a promise to him that I would do my very best at raising our boys. I knew I could never replace him or be that role model in their life, but I promised to do the best that I could.

I exited the truck and went back inside and cried some more. I did not leave my room except for doing what I had to for the next two weeks. I could not process all of the deaths at one time. I could only process my daughter at first. I realized at this time I was starting to process Dustin's. I felt a very heavy burden knowing I could not fill his shoes and mine.

It is these burdens and such things that our heavenly Father wants us to give to Him. Knowing these things are out of our control and in His control.

As time went on, things began to worsen with Payton's father. I accepted there would be no wedding. What reason was there to keep the relationship going forward? I began to think it was time to go.

CHAPTER 3

Listening to God and Making Good Decisions in Our Lives

Coming up on one year since Jesus decided to take Brooke and Dustin home, I struggled with making a final decision. The choice to end my current relationship and start co-parenting again. I didn't want to live with regret. The deep need to be able to say that I did everything that I could do held me back. Payton remained forefront in my decision. I didn't want another child to have to go through all the emotions a broken home brought. And what about my other children? Even though we weren't married, it would affect them. Another broken family situation. And what would people say?

So many times in life we suffer and stay in situations based on concern over what others might think or say, not trusting in God that He will make a way. As humans, we are not made perfect.

I have said so many times that God only made one Jesus and thank heaven He did. We are all flawed and make mistakes, and the ones who act as if they aren't are living a lie. Sometimes we get ourselves into messes, but God always makes a way out. Now, that doesn't mean there aren't consequences for our actions—because there definitely are. But we thank Jesus for His everlasting love and grace. He forgives us and helps us always when we run to Him. In fact, that's what He longs for us to do.

I was in my room one night, contemplating, and it was as if I heard Dustin's voice saying, "You can do this… You had the strength and the courage to leave me, and we had three children together. You can do it again."

Dustin was right.

As beat down as I was, as humbled as I was, as broken as I was, God gave me the strength to make the best decision for mine and my children's sake. He carried me through it every heartache, every struggle, and He would continue to. From that day and that point on, I took my engagement ring off, laid down my worries, and I did it. With God, I did it!

That relationship was not God's plan for my life—it was my plan and my plan led me down a road of destruction.

God gave me a very precious gift out of my lack of obedience that I will forever be grateful for, and her name is Payton, my little saving grace. This gift, such a precious child, I will forever be grateful for.

That December, my mother asked me what size ring I wore and I told her, thinking in the back of my mind she must be buying me a ring for Christmas. My mom, like most grandmothers, once asked Brooke which of her jewelry she wanted to one day inherit. Brooke selected a ring she specifically loved—the engagement ring my dad had given my mother.

That Christmas, my mom sized that ring to fit me as a gift. What a special present, one I will always cherish. I had taken my engagement ring off, and this one replaced it. That ring represented three of the dearest people to my heart. One of the best Christmas gifts I had ever gotten.

My children and I just held on to each other, trusting in Jesus to take care of us. One day at a time. Every night when my head hit the pillow, I thanked God for his many blessings—for just getting me through the day.

That Christmas, we put up a special tree for Brooke and invited all of her friends to place an ornament on it. The ornaments were all so beautiful. Now I enjoy putting the tree up every year. Such a sweet reminder of how much she was loved.

We marked the one-year anniversary of her passing. It was like reliving the day all over again. Every year, so far, it seems to be that way. Like when your child has a birthday and you can think back to every detail of the day they came into this world, every detail of their birth, and every detail of that joy. It is the same way when you have lost one. You think of every detail of that awful day, every detail of their death, every detail of the sorrow and sadness.

I had friends surrounding me. They even spent the night with me the first year. I am so thankful for their support and their love.

I found myself wanting to give back to other families every Christmas thereafter, something that helped keep me very busy throughout the season. I believe the more we do for others can be very therapeutic, and it brings me pure joy. I pray to have a servant heart daily.

For two years, I created paintings and Christmas ornaments by hand. Some you will see named the same as the titles of the parts in this book. One was a painting of baby Jesus in a manger, another an ornament of baby Jesus, and the last an angel. They were titled "How I Survived, My Saving Grace, and Bringing Light to the Loss." I sold them and used the proceeds to help families in a season of need at Christmas.

The first year this took place, I went through a radio station called 107 - The Fish and picked the most precious family. I stayed up all night long, painting for hours. A type of therapy for me and so relaxing. I really enjoyed it. I remember contacting the mother of this sweet family and asking her what types of things her children liked. She proceeded to tell me about her son. She said he liked trucks, but he really liked airplanes. I paused and took a deep breath. Now was the time to tell her Brooke's story and how all of this began. My heart sank for a minute. But I pulled myself together and began to explain about my sweet Brookie.

I believe paths cross for a reason, not by coincidence. When an opportunity arises or a door opens, I don't hesitate to share my story. This family holds a special place in my heart, and I will never forget them.

CHAPTER 4

Where She Met Jesus

In March of 2013, we had our school spring break, and I really wanted to visit the crash site in Texas. I wanted to see the place where my daughter met Jesus. I also wanted to meet the people who found them and did everything they could to help them. I often thought about them and what it must have been like to have witnessed the crash and how it might have affected them long-term. When we see things like that, it is forever embedded in our brain. Such things people never forget.

I remember searching for answers and researching everything I could. I listened to the 911 call. To the radio contact between Dustin and the air traffic controller up until they completely lost contact. Dustin sounded so calm and in control, but knowing him as I did, I could also detect a hint of nervousness in his voice.

I wanted to go to the ranch where this happened and have them take me to the place where they found Brooke. I needed to see these things to move forward. I also wanted the families there to know the people they found, and how great they were.

I started planning the trip. It was me, my children, one of my girlfriends, and a friend at the time, Robbie. Robbie and I went to high school together and were reunited by some really good friends of ours that February. He is a former Marine and said he would drive the RV to Texas for us, which made me feel more comfortable with my kids traveling with us. We'd talked on the phone every day from the time we were reunited, and I sensed there was something very special about him.

I set out to find an RV to rent for spring break. I contacted the family who owned the ranch in Texas, and we planned our trip. I prayed that God would show me something on this trip. I will have to admit, the trip was bittersweet. I loved having my family so close, but the reason for visiting wasn't pleasant. But it was important to me to get a clearer picture of what might have happened on that night.

Our first stop was in Mississippi. We stayed at a campsite right across the street from the beach, which I loved. It was so nice. My boys cooked waffles on the grill that next morning. The shore was so pretty. My girlfriend and I laughed a lot, and Payton loved the playground. Robbie made sure we were all taken care of. We watched movies at night and all of us sat up talking until the wee hours of the morning.

Our next stop was Louisiana. Dustin has family there, so we stopped by and visited, then stayed a night at the campground nearby. This campsite could only be described as quirky. My girlfriend picked this one, and we found lots to laugh about there. So many good memories were made. The next day, we would travel on to Texas.

That morning, anxiety and nervousness filled me. I wanted so much to find answers. I made the family in Texas a gift basket with Georgia things. For example, a kudzu candle, a vine that grows wild all over Georgia. The scent is unique, sweet like candy with the fragrance of tropical fruits and berries. I also made them some homemade goodies. I included a copy of the funeral program for each person on the plane. I wanted them to know what they looked like and how great each and every one of them were. I also wanted them to know that they were in heaven and more alive than we are.

As we headed out that morning, we made one stop at the mall. My boys wanted to get some new shoes. We had some time to kill, so we hung out there for a little while. The drive was so pretty, the land beautiful. All the lovely farms. What was life like for them?

When we finally arrived, I remember looking around and thinking to myself...*wow, this is it.* My stomach knotted, but I knew there had to be something or some kind of answer there.

As we unloaded from the RV, we were greeted by one of the sweetest families, who I will always cherish in my heart. They'd done everything they could to help our loved ones and they were so accommodating to me.

We greeted each other, and I introduced myself. I presented them with their gift basket, and I acquainted them with each of the passengers—who they were and how we were all related.

Then the time came for me to see exactly where the crash took place. They described to me what they encountered that night—the sound, the loud boom, the darkness that made it impossible to see anything. The debris scattered a mile long, and many parts of the plane strewn in different areas.

As we walked through an open field, they took me to where the plane nosedived and eventually landed. The engine had been buried in the ground. I just can't imagine walking out of your house and finding such devastation. Not to mention the days that followed, filled with news crews, investigators, and police.

How often I had thought about these things. Who the family and the young gentleman who actually found them were... What the area looked like... What went on that night? The gentleman kindly explained what details he could. I had already seen the plane on the news, so I had an idea.

Then came the time to ask the big question. "Where did you find my daughter?"

"Not far. Just right over here on the other side of these trees." We walked over to the exact place where he found her.

I can't describe what I felt looking at the ground where her lifeless body once lay. I can't explain the feeling that came over me. *This very place, this place that I am standing, is where my baby girl met Jesus.*

I just stared at the ground, having flashes in my mind of what the scene must have looked like on the night of December 19th, 2011. If it were just me there that day, I might have laid down on the ground where she was found and sobbed, but I held it in for everyone around me.

It started to rain. It also rained the night of the crash. I so wanted everyone to just walk away so I could hit my knees and cry out to God. To scream out WHY, but when the rain came, it was as if I could hear Brooke saying, "Enough. Enough, Momma, I am not there." As if she were telling me, "It is time for you to go." Lightning began to zap across the sky, so we headed back to the barn.

As I'd planned this trip, I'd convinced myself something amazing was going to happen—something extraordinary or miraculous. This family was so kind to let us visit. I shared with them that Brooke's cell was the only phone not sent back and that we were texting each other that night. I believed it was still out there somewhere and asked them to keep an eye out. You know how teenagers are—they always have their phones with them. I believe she was holding it as the plane went down. They promised they would keep an eye out.

When I left there, it may not have seemed like anything particularly notable had happened, but I met a wonderful family who I will cherish forever, and I left there having peace without having all the answers.

CHAPTER 5

Time to Stop Searching

Sometimes in life we are not going to have all the answers. We could search and search, but I believe that there are some things we are just not supposed to know. I also believe if the timing isn't right, God has a way of waiting, until we are ready, to reveal things. There are things about the crash that I may never know, and I have found a place where I am okay with that. What I do know is what really matters and that is where my loved ones are now. I am assured that I will get to spend eternity with them one day because of Jesus and his sacrifice. That, my friends, is where I find my peace. *Thank you, Jesus, for what you did for me, for all of us, on that cross that day. I am so undeserving but so grateful that you loved all of us so much that you would die so that we could live forever.*

I did leave the ranch that day with peace. I felt as though Brooke had wanted me to know and see the place where she met Jesus, but knowing where she ended up was way more important than where she met him.

I chose not to stay in Texas that night. I wanted to head back to Louisiana. The rest of the trip, a quietness lingered, except for the last day, which happened to be Easter.

I'd made Easter baskets for everyone and my girlfriend and I cooked a ham with a big dinner in the RV. A certain happiness seemed to dance in my children that day, a lightness. Robbie and I spent time together, and we got to know each other better. What a great guy he was to come along and volunteer to drive so all this could be possible. I am forever glad he shared this experience with my family.

We headed back to Georgia. We had a memorial race to plan for in May. That always kept me busy for the month of April. This year's race was called the color run, and it would become one of my favorites.

When we returned from Texas, I knew in my heart that there would be no more investigating or trying to figure out the crash. I just took a second to be still and look around me. I recognized how much people loved my daughter and my family.

Isn't it crazy how we can become so immune to dysfunction surrounding us and unhealthy relationships? We let it become our lives and eventually that is our new normal and all that we know. A vicious cycle that just keeps repeating if we don't wake up and start making wise choices.

All my life, I tended to move from one dysfunction to the next. I wanted out of the hamster wheel so badly I would find myself in another negative situation just trying to save myself from the last one. If someone nice, kind, loving, and faithful came my way, I pushed them away, thinking them too good to be true or that it was all a front. I had lost trust in everyone.

Robbie proved himself a good man frequently, but I wasn't ready for any kind of dating. I'd grown numb and found myself at a place where I was just done with men and relationships altogether. I told God all I needed was Him. My family and Jesus. There was no man on earth going to love me the way Jesus does. So I quit searching for that kind of love. I set my expectations too high. Remember how I said that there is only one Jesus? Only one perfect man. We are all flawed and very imperfect and we must show grace and realize that other people are also not perfect.

Robbie gave me space because I asked for it. I felt as though that was fair to him. I did miss his company, but the best thing he could have done was exactly what he did—he gave me the time and space I needed and asked for. It made me respect him that much more. We talked on the phone occasionally, but we did not see as much of one another.

That May was the Brooke Butler Memorial Color Run. It was always the weekend of Mother's Day, which I absolutely loved because moms and their kids would come out and run together.

We all went out to eat for Mother's Day. My sister visited and spent the night with me and ran in the race. Robbie also came and even brought along his parents in support of myself, my family, and the race.

I knew Robbie was a good man. I just didn't know if I had anything left in me to offer him. I didn't want to let him go, but I didn't want to be selfish either. I'd never had someone be so genuine and kind to me. There was just one problem and one question I had for God.

CHAPTER 6

To New Beginnings

As I sat in my room one night, I said to God, "God, why would you send me such a great man when I have nothing to offer him? I am broken and numb. I don't have anything left in me to give. I poured so much of myself, my time, my love, and my spirit into the wrong relationships. I tried to change people to be what I needed them to be. I'm always trying to see all the good and potential in people, but so the end results are always disappointing."

I went on, "God, it would not be fair to him to be in a relationship with me."

Then I heard God speak to my heart. "My child," he said, "I have sent him so you can experience love and how it feels to be loved by someone who respects and adores you. It's your time now. You just love him the best you know how and leave the rest up to me."

Every night, I prayed God would love Robbie through me, and He did. I grew to adore this man, respect him and honor him, but I did not put him before Jesus. As I've said before—there is no greater love than the love of Jesus Christ. We, as humans, our flesh cannot give that kind of love. We can only ask Him to give it through us.

Robbie and I had both been married and divorced. We spoke of marriage often and what we would expect of a husband and a wife. Then one day we talked specifically about *us* getting married. We were joking around and laughing and we said why we don't make our last names the same? I just looked at him in awe and thought to myself, "Why don't we?"

When Robbie started talking about going to look at rings, I looked at the one already on my finger. The ring my mom had given me. That my dad had given her and that Brooke eventually wanted. How precious would it be to use that ring? I asked Robbie if we could use the diamond and have the rest designed. Everyone who the ring represented I put on a pedestal and held so dear to my heart. Of course, he agreed.

We sat down with the jeweler designing the ring. Because it reminded me of so many people, I wanted my diamond to sit high, so I needed high prongs. So many people who I love reflected in that stone and thus the diamond needed to stand tall like the pedestal I placed them all on.

On July 30, 2013, the sweetest thing happened. Robbie took all of us, the kids included, to a place called Stone Mountain. There, one can walk to the top of this huge mountain and look out. I wore a pair of Brooke's shoes. We often shared shoes and clothes, and I still did. We all climbed to the very top, even little Payton, three years old at the time. At the very top is where he asked me to be his wife. He explained that he wanted to bring me as close to Brooke and my father as he could. How thoughtful! I'd never had someone love me this way. When we got into the car, I made a video on my phone about it.

We started planning a wedding for May of 2014. I wanted to get married in Tennessee, where my father was from, because I absolutely love the mountains. We found a beautiful venue called White Stone

Country Inn, with breathtaking views and an unreal peace about it. The gorgeous chapel was just perfect.

I wanted to get married in a house of God. God was at the center of this relationship, and I intended to center my marriage around Him as well. Something I hadn't done before. I wanted my marriage to be blessed, and I wanted it to last.

I can honestly assure you, hands down, if you keep God at the center of your marriage, it will not fail. It takes both partners though, not just one, to make a marriage work. Sometimes it takes a lot of effort and time to get two people on the same page. I am not saying that your marriage will not be blessed if it doesn't take place in a chapel, but that is just where I felt closer to Jesus at the time.

Sometimes I feel closer to him by the creek at my house, but a chapel is a Holy place to me and for the start of this marriage, I needed that. All I wanted was to feel His presence, His blessing, as we entered into this promise together. He will meet you wherever you are if you just call on Him. He is a loving father.

We worked through pre-marriage counseling at the church and stayed very busy making things and putting our vision together. So many things to prepare for and figure out: the dress, the flowers, the food, the cake, the guests, the invitations, and photographers. So much goes into that one special day and it is over in a blink of an eye. I have to say, it was so much fun planning and doing those things together because I am one who loves to decorate and plan a gathering or a party.

It was in the stillness of the night, when the day would end and everything was so quiet, I would start thinking. Who will walk me down the aisle? My maid of honor couldn't be present—she was in heaven. I so badly wanted to share this precious day with her. We used to talk about it, even. I just knew she would be enjoying this if she could be here.

Let me tell you a funny little story. A few years prior to Brooke's passing, we were shopping and went to Victoria's Secret. While browsing, we found this robe on display, and on the back of it in rhinestones, the word BRIDE glittered. As I gazed at its glamour and beauty, I dreamed of the day that I would marry again. I glanced at Brooke and she said, with her cute little personality, "Mom, you're not getting married," and giggled.

"Oh, but I will one day... So I am getting it."

We both laughed and laughed.

There was another time when we were crafting together and started making bouquets, which morphed into a bridal bouquet. Brooke glued all the beautiful jewels on. Okay, ya'll, can you see God working in that moment? Do you see what He was doing? What was taking place at that very moment? There was no wedding planned, no reason for us to be doing that, but He allowed her to be a part of my wedding because He knew. She was a part of it all through Jesus.

If I had not acted on those silly times, making those memories, I would not have had those precious gems on my wedding day. The things that I would carry, her hands had touched and even made.

The big day inched closer, filled with joyous preparation and palpable excitement. For wedding favors, Robbie and I made a batch of homemade jelly and together we put our personal touch on all the table decorations, invitations, save-the-dates, and so on. How perfectly everything seemed to come together. And, yet, I felt as if I couldn't escape the huge void that a part of me was missing.

I decided to ask my niece, one of Brooke's cousins on her father's side, and two of her friends who were both born on the third of a month, like Brooke, to be in my wedding. My niece would be my maid of honor, who would carry a memorial candle. The other girls carried the flowers that Brooke would have held, and a picture of her, and they placed them on a table where she would have stood. Then they all lit the candle in remembrance.

I chose to get married on May 3, Brooke's birthday. The date I became a parent and that my parents became grandparents. A day full of love. A great day. So why not marry my best friend on that very date as well?

Robbie agreed it was a great idea, so with our wedding date decided, we moved on to the next big question. Who would give me away?

We also included a memorial candle that my sister and my mom lit in memory of my father. I decided to ask my boys to walk me down the aisle. We stick together through everything, as family should, and who better than the young men at the center of my life?

The weekend arrived quickly. Before we left, I needed to visit the cemetery. It is such a quiet place, a place where I could just take it all in. I often went there to talk to her. I changed her flowers every month, determined to keep everything nice for her friends when they visited. After all, don't we do that for our kids here on earth? Clean their room and make sure things are presentable? I continued to do so for her. It was just a different place to visit.

That day, I confided in her, "I'm a little nervous, so be with me this weekend. I will be back soon to visit." As I started to walk away and head back to Dustin's truck, which I currently drove because I needed to keep it up and running for Jacob when he turned sixteen, it was as if I felt her walking behind me. As if I heard her little voice saying, "Okay, Momma, we can come back here and all later. It looks really pretty. I mean I love the flowers and all, but I am coming with you. Yes, I said coming with you to Tennessee to see you get married. I am not here in some grave. I am in heaven. Alive, very alive." I smiled and the tears started flowing—happy tears, because I knew how true all of that was, and sad tears, because I couldn't physically see her beautiful face.

I also thought about Dustin. If he could have handpicked a man to raise his boys, knowing that he couldn't, he would pick someone just like Robbie to set that example for them.

I believe we'll all have duties in heaven. I believe they're working all the time on things and rejoicing. If you slow down enough and really look at things around you—the events, big and small, that take place in your life—you can witness these little miracles with your own eyes.

Friday, May 2, we were all packed up and headed to Tennessee. Anxious, excited, and nervous all-in-one.

Everything went according to plan, and the celebration was beautiful. I could not have asked for more. We had our loved ones, family, and friends surrounding us for that very special day. It was a true blessing to pledge our love in front of them and God. We stayed a wonderful two nights and returned home on Sunday the fifth.

CHAPTER 7

A True Miracle…

As we drove home from Tennessee that Sunday, I received a text from the family in Texas. They asked what kind of cell phone Brooke had. I couldn't even text them back. I had to call them! I described her white iPhone, an early Christmas present.

They'd found one matching that very description. As they were working on a fence, they looked down and there it was—a white iPhone right at their feet. It'd been crushed, but they would put it in the mail the very next day, a Monday.

I received it that Wednesday. Oh, how I remember opening that package. I couldn't tear it open it fast enough, and sure enough, there was her white iPhone—crushed, shattered, and full of dirt. The back was pried open and there was dried mud packed all in it. It sat out in the hot Texas weather through storms and heat and cold for two and a half years. Would anything even work on it?

But I was just happy to have her phone—the last thing that her hands probably touched. I saw it as a miracle it was even found, although deep inside me, I just knew it was out there. That they would find it one day. To hold it in my hands and to touch the last thing that she touched—I can't even explain what that felt like.

In Hebrews 11:1 the Bible says, *Now faith is confidence in what we hope for and assurance about what we do not see.* It goes on to say in Matthew 17:20, *If you have faith as small as a mustard seed, you can say to this mountain, "Move from here to there," and it will move. Nothing will be impossible for you.*

We took the phone to a local business in my hometown called Cell Tech in hopes that there might be something they could recover. The nice gentlemen explained to Robbie and me with a look of doubt that there "might" be a ten percent chance that we could get anything. By the looks of the phone, the situation seemed pretty hopeless. But, he would try.

He took the phone in the back to start to work on it. Sometime later, he came back out and told me he was able to remove all of the dirt. So he went back and continued to work on the phone. A little while longer passed, and he came back out a second time. "There's no rust on this phone. The dirt must have saved it from that." I couldn't believe it. The dirt literally saved it from rusting. He declared we were now at twenty percent of recovering something. He left again to work on it a bit, then came back and announced, "We can raise that to thirty percent." He kept repeating, "I just can't believe it!"

He returned with the phone in his hand and said, "Look her brightness was turned all the way up."

"Yes, I figured it would be, considering that they were flying at night."

"It's a miracle that this phone works at all. A true miracle!"

He came out once more. "The only thing we need now is her password."

My heart sank as I looked at him. "I don't know. It was an early Christmas present, and she just got it before she left."

Panic edged in. Had we come this far just to hit a wall?

"That's okay. I have a way around it. This will take a while so I will call you in the morning, and let you know what I can retrieve off of it."

It was five, so closing time was upon us, and Robbie and I needed to go and pick up a few things from the store. I thanked him for all he'd done and told him I would talk to him the next day and we left.

Not even an hour later, my phone rang while we were in the store, and I recognized the voice immediately. The gentlemen at the phone place! He exclaimed, "Alison, I got it! I got everything! I was able to get her texts, pictures, and everything."

My heart skipped a beat. I took a deep breath and responded with awe and gratefulness, "You did? I will be there first thing in the morning to pick it up."

The next morning, I hurried to pick up the phone. He'd saved everything on a jump drive. When I walked in, he wore a look on his face. I sensed he wanted to tell me something and he did. "Alison, there's a message in her drafts that she was not able to send, and it's to you."

Again, my heart skipped a beat, and I took a deep breath. Her last message. The last things she thought and typed were to me, but she could not send them. The possible answer to the questions I'd carried in the back of my mind. Did she know? Was it instant? Was she afraid?

CHAPTER 8

Her Last Words

I needed to see the message. I could not wait until I got home. The suspense would kill me. I explained this to the gentleman at Cell Tech, and he responded with understanding. He took me to his computer and suggested, "You might want to sit down."

So many thoughts ran rampant through my mind. What were her last words?

Nervousness, anxiousness, and even a little fear swirled through me. As I sat, he pulled up the text left in the drafts folder.

Dad said we are crashing so scrd I love you mo. She abbreviated scared, and she could not put the last m on mom. Her little fingers could not even hit send.

I just gasped for air as tears ran down my face. Even now, as I write this, the tears flow at the thought of it. My sweet, sweet girl…scared, afraid, and aware they were crashing… And I was not there to help her to calm her, to hold her, or to tell her that I loved her one last time.

I gathered my things and expressed my deep appreciation to the man who'd helped me so much. I just wanted to get home to my safe place where I could process all of this.

I just kept dwelling on all of them knowing—aware they would crash—that it was not instant. Then I thought to myself, if I were in a car and about to be in an accident and saw it coming, I would try to brace myself or hold on. I don't know what was said on that plane, but I am sure they expressed their love—and who knows what else? What I do know is that our heavenly father was there to comfort them all.

The local news station heard about the phone. I still do not know until this day how, but I didn't mind. They did a story on it because what better story than a true miracle? But I did not want them including the part about Brooke knowing they were crashing. I asked that they only talk about the second half of the message, *I love you mo.*

That weekend, ironically, was Mother's Day and we had the Brooke Butler Memorial Race. I needed to remain positive. I felt as though Brooke were saying, "Here is my phone, Mom. I know you wanted it. I love you, and I am okay. Happy Mother's Day."

God shows us how real He is in situations like this. That they found the phone alone was pure miracle. That it worked, another miracle.

God wants us to get to know Him, to long for Him, and to love Him. His timing is everything.

Had I received that text on the night of the crash, I would not have been able to handle it. God revealed these things two and a half years later. On His timing, at the right time. When I could handle it.

In everything, God has a purpose. He has a plan. Even in the hardest times of our lives. All of this was part of His plan. He even takes the bad decisions that we make and still makes a way for us. Now don't get me wrong—there are definitely consequences for our actions, but He is still there. He will reveal Himself to us if we allow Him to. We have to be willing to learn and to obey.

Throughout my life, God has blessed me with several miracles. He has picked me up from rock bottom many times. He has shown His mercy on me and given me grace through my mistakes. He loves us so much. He will do whatever it takes to draw close to us, and so, I will do whatever it takes to be close to Him. He is my desire—no one else will do. Nothing will ever take His place. One of my favorite songs included this chorus.

You're all I want
You're all I ever needed
You're all I want
Help me know you are near.

In this next section, I hope to show you that it is not always easy to be a Christian. Putting God first can be challenging. It can be a lonely place at times. But once you understand there is a plan, it is all worth it.

FROM REJECTED
TO REDEEMED

CHAPTER 1

The Lonely Place

Busyness filled the next few years as well as a lot of movement and transformation. I still wasn't completely healed, but I knew my job was to listen, read God's word, and be obedient.

Again, I found myself in a lonely place. I felt as if my story scared people and for some, it probably did. I found friends disappearing, not being able to handle who I'd become. I grew very vocal about my spirituality and how God saved me.

I also asked God to weed out the people in my life who did not need to be there. Any "toxic relationships" as we commonly refer to them today. He sure weeded them out alright. I found myself asking, "God, why did you bring me to this place in my life to be alone?"

Often, as I sat in the stillness and quiet, reading my Bible by myself, I would wait on God to speak. Of course, I never heard God's literal voice—when I say speak to me, it means speak to my heart.

If you don't understand what I mean by that, it's the little voice in your head that tells you that you shouldn't do something. Or the whisper in the back of your mind cautioning, "This is not good." In that same way, He can speak to your heart. You just need to listen.

So one day He laid this truth on my heart. *I work better through you alone. You are too distracted by people and things to do what you have been called to.*

So many people have judged me. And aren't people always going to have something to say? Either you are not grieving enough or you are grieving too much. How can you smile and look so happy, some asked. But if I were down all the time, they'd say, "Bless her heart, she'll never be the same." I was unfriended by many, even one of Brooke's closest friends. I even had someone come up to me at a celebration and ask, "How can you be so happy when there is such a huge piece missing?"

They had no idea part of the reason I tried to keep it together was for them. And that wasn't easy, putting my feelings on the back burner. Pushing through all of the firsts, just to be a part of their lives. You can always tell, at the end of the day, who your true friends are. And I could tell who Brooke's were, because they stayed very close to me. Those who knew her understood how close Brooke and I were and that Brooke would want it that way.

I also would say this—if people would draw close to God, then they would understand how I could smile. It wasn't easy, but I was always one who hated crying in front of people. I had my certain friends with whom I would do that with, and they would just be there and listen and comfort me.

It is Jesus who saved me and Jesus who carried me. His words tell me where my family is and it is a wonderful place, so yes, that actually does put a smile on my face. My Brooke is in the best hands—the hands of our Almighty Powerful Loving Father. The One who gives us life, and the One who carries us when we feel as if we are dying.

The One who breathes life into you, and the One who carries us home to be with Him. The One who, no matter what we do, has mercy on us and loves us anyway. The only One who can give us eternal life to spend with Him and our loved ones. He loves us so much that He died a cruel torturing death so we could live for eternity.

The Bible says, *You will fill me with joy in your presence.* Psalm 16:11

I long for His presence daily. After the crash, I hungered to learn everything about heaven. I wanted to understand more about Jesus and be as close to Him as I could. He is my lifeline.

I found the closer I drew to Him, relationships started to vanish. I had a friend warn me this would happen. She said, "When things settle, everyone will go back to living life like nothing happened, but for you it will stay." This relationship, ironically, vanished as well.

The truth is just too much for some people. I no longer lived in this bubble, but found myself on the outside. I felt as though I did not fit in anywhere. As if no one understood me except Jesus.

CHAPTER 2

People and Their Expectations

I began to share my story in the hope someone would understand, only to find myself disappointed again with the reactions I received. People who I expected would show me grace failed to. I often felt judged. Some acted as if I'd contracted a disease or something. I was still me, after all, but so many seemed to place impossible standards for me…or just didn't want to deal with me.

Over time, I realized I set my expectations way too high. Ironically, the people who disappointed me the most were Christians. Why? Perhaps I also set my hopes too high for even so-called Godly persons.

But we are all human, and if we put too much expectation and trust in people, we're bound to be let down. To find ourselves disappointed. I often told people, "Please don't expect a lot from me because I will fail you at this time in my life. I just don't have a lot left to give." The only One who will never fail you is Jesus.

I recently heard some wise words from Tyler Perry, that he posted on his Instagram, that said; "There are people that come in your life, sometimes, to be there for a season. They weren't meant to be there always. Sometimes, we find ourselves hooked up with people that we think are there for a lifetime, but they were only supposed to be there for a season. There are people who come in your life like boosters for a rocket. If you ever watch a rocket going to space, the boosters fall off, when it reaches a certain altitude. Some people are not equipped to handle the altitudes that you're going to. So don't be afraid when they fall off, they're not bad people. They just couldn't go where you're going." His words gave me a better understanding of our relationships, with people throughout our life.

Now, I sought joy in different things in my life. Oh, the void remains present, and how I wish Brooke were here still to experience things with me. But I feel she's here in some way. Just not where I can see her. I believe when we rejoice on earth they also rejoice in heaven.

After the crash, my boys were baptized. How I wished their father and sister were there to witness it. At the service, I closed my eyes, tears running down my face. I could almost feel the overwhelming joy, the dancing, the chanting, and the power of the presence of Jesus. I believe that is what they were doing in heaven. Everyone was so happy there.

Let's talk about happiness. There were times I asked myself, will I ever be happy again? Really happy, not just moments here and there? And where I was looking for happiness? In people? In my children? My spouse? I realized that was a defeating source to chase. To find happiness in people can't work, because people will always let you down in some way. We are not perfect and others are not responsible for our happiness. We alone are responsible for our happiness. It is a choice. I could decide if I was going to be happy or not. If I didn't feel happy that day I had to learn to give myself grace and realize not every day is full of joy.

The only true fulfillment is in the Lord. He will complete all the areas in which we feel are lacking. When we turn to Him about our disappointments, He guides us and speaks to us and He loves us. He reminds us that we are all just people who make mistakes. He might even remind us of our own mistakes and the grace He has given us when we may have disappointed others or even ourselves. I know He has humbled me on more than one occasion.

I went to a person one time who I looked at as a role model. I still admire this person, but what she said I didn't quite know how to take. I felt misunderstood, disappointed, and let down. I felt rejected.

My story is one that really scares people. I often feel no one understands me. Constantly rejected. So I tell myself I just needed to shut my mouth.

Now *that* sounds like something straight from the enemy, if you ask me. After reading my written words back to myself, I realized what better way to destroy me than to make me feel worthless, alone, and rejected?

The enemy does not want us to keep pressing on. He does not want us to succeed. He does not want us to be obedient. He wants to tear you down, manipulate you, and make you feel like you are nothing. If he can get you low enough with his lies to the point of hopelessness, he has got you. He has destroyed you enough to lead you to fall back into your old ways, deceitfulness, and backslidden life. Then you feel even worse about yourself. We have all been there. It has happened to all of us at least once in our life. That is why he is here—he is on a mission to kill, steal, and destroy.

Oh, but we serve a mighty God! The word says, "'Vengeance is his,' saith the Lord." This verse reminds us who we are up against. When we feel rejected, hopeless, and depressed, we must rise above and say, "Not today, Satan. God says I am great. My God says I am somebody. My God says I can do it, and I don't care if I have to go alone, I will be obedient. I am going to follow Jesus no matter how many friends I lose, and no matter how many people judge me." Because in the end there is no one, and I mean no one, like our God.

He has carried me, He has believed in me, He was who I cried out to and shouted "save me" to over and over again. He has always been there when no one else was, and He has never failed me.

He was there when my baby almost drowned, He was there when terror shook my daughter, and He was there when my daddy felt no hope. When my first husband felt he had no control. In abusive relationships. Through the divorce and through all of the loss. He has always been there and still is lifting me up off of my knees when I feel as though I just can't take another step or handle another thing.

To us, what seems like rejection could be God leading us in a different direction. The breakup that you thought you couldn't get over, could really be a breakthrough. Sometimes, I think God's protection can appear to look like rejection to us.

Don't lose sight of who is in control. Always remember your self-worth. You are a gem, a precious soul who God created for a purpose.

CHAPTER 3

Redeemed

I was rejected but redeemed. People rejected me, left me, turned their back on me, talked about me, judged me...but I kept reminding myself that people treated Jesus terribly and He loved them anyway. I am redeemed.

Thank You, Jesus, for saving me! Thank You, Jesus, for redeeming me! Thank You, Jesus, for removing those toxic people in my life who would have held me back from my purpose! Thank You, Jesus, for loving someone like me!

One particular day, as we were sitting in my kitchen, a friend said to me, "You need to write a book."

I just looked at her and laughed. I thought to myself, *I should write a book? Yeah right!*

I just smiled and answered, "Really? I wouldn't even know where to begin."

"Just start writing."

This conversation took place in 2014, and I just tucked the thought away in the back of my mind. I could never write a book.

After Robbie and I married, I knew he wanted to try for a child of his own. We discussed it many times. And my boys so badly wanted another little brother. It had to be a boy, of course! I reminded them that you can't choose if it is a boy or a girl. God always gives you what you need.

I was really nervous about this because after the loss, my body truly felt about ten years older on the inside. The stress of it all took a major toll on me. At one point, I even lost my hair, which thankfully God gave back to me. Was I healthy enough? Could I do this? Physically *and* emotionally?

I was thirty-seven years old when I spoke with my doctor about the possibility. His advice was to try sooner rather than later—not to wait until after I turned forty. I went home and explained to Robbie, and we started trying to have our fifth baby.

By January of 2015, we were all very excited to find out what the gender of the baby was. At that time, you could find out as early as thirteen weeks. I will never forget that phone call that day from the doctor. She said everything looked good and asked me if I wanted to know what I was having. I said, "Yes, I want to know!"

"You are having a little boy," she revealed. Our family was blessed with a nine-pound little bundle of joy on October 1, 2015. We named him Barrett.

CHAPTER 4

When Things Are Out of Your Control

A few days after I came home from the hospital, I noticed my heart beat very slowly. Something just didn't feel right. I went to the emergency room. They checked my vitals and then asked me if I was a runner. I explained I just had a baby via a C-section.

My heart rate was at forty and my blood pressure was 175 over 85. My blood pressure was 110 over 60 on a normal day. I sat in the waiting room scared and panicked.

They brought in an older lady by ambulance and wheeled her right next to me. She looked at me, and I looked at her. It was as if our eyes just connected. This scared me even more. My mind went straight to a book I'd read. In that book, God appears as a woman. For some reason, this lady reminded me of that.

Suddenly, I feared death so much it became palpable. I wasn't ready. I just had a baby. My children needed me. God spoke to my heart. *Do you think Dustin was ready at the age of thirty-three? Or Brooke, at only fourteen? This is out of your control.*

They came and took the women back. I paced the hallway and called one of my friends. Terror filled me, but for the first time in my life, I accepted I was not in control of anything in my life. Only God is. A feeling of relief washed over me as I dwelled on that reality. As mothers, we try to control things to protect everyone around us. We try to shield our children, ourselves, our husbands, our entire family. It is just our nature, but in doing so, we carry a heavy weight that is not meant for us.

A really bad headache set in, then I started throwing up. They treated me for postpartum hypertension and sent me home. I prayed to God that He would heal me, and He did. I was better in a matter of two weeks.

One night as I lay in bed, about an hour after I had fallen asleep, I heard God whisper in my heart. He wanted me to write and for me to get into the Word (the Bible). Meaning read it, learn it. We must have knowledge and know Him through His Word as well as have an intimate relationship with Him.

In my mind, I vowed to be faithful and do whatever He asked of me. But, I asked him to prepare the way and guide me—because I had no idea what I was doing.

CHAPTER 5

When God Speaks, You Obey

That November, I started writing. Not on a computer, but in a journal my friend gifted me. On the cover, it said, "Write." And so I did.

I began to get a feeling from God that change was coming—movement—and not just within me, or our family life, but all over the world. It was time for me to move and to start packing. To start cleaning out my house.

Over the next year, I poured myself into this effort, although I didn't quite understand why. The task was overwhelming, Where to start? What to keep and what to giveaway? I had a lot of work ahead of me. My basement was full from ceiling to floor with all of Dustin's and Brooke's things.

A person's steps are directed by the Lord. How then can anyone understand their own way? Proverbs 20:24

Somehow, I knew it was time. Time for yet another change in my life, but this time would prove different. This time I had chosen to follow Jesus.

I began cleaning things out of my upstairs and two months later our basement flooded. I couldn't avoid that task now. I said, "Okay, God, here we go!" Sometimes I think He helps us along the way to get our rear in gear.

That was one way to put a pep in our step. We cleaned the basement out, fixed the foundation, and that next January we spoke to our amazing realtor. She had the house on the market by that June.

In the meantime, we started looking for our new home. I frequently found houses and rode by them to see if they would be a good fit. While I loved the majority of the houses we looked at, there was this one. I had already vowed to God that I only wanted to be where *He* wanted my family to be. I asked Him to make His presence known in this place—if it were the one.

We went back and forth with the seller. I told Robbie not to go back to him with any more offers. If we forced it, how could we see God in it? Needless to say, the deal did not work out. And praise God! It wasn't where we were meant to be.

We continued looking. My frustration grew. Where would we live? When would we find it? I've often found myself asking such questions throughout my life. It's so easy to expect things on our timing and suffer disappointment. God frequently reminds me that His timing is the only way to do things...not mine.

Oh, how great are God's riches and wisdom and knowledge! How impossible it is for us to understand His decisions and His ways! Romans 11:33

CHAPTER 6

Our Ways are Not His Ways

If I receive a vision from God, a dream, or even when He just reveals His presence to me, I'm excited. I want to tell everyone about it! For a while, I assumed all believers experienced such things. And to share them is to give Him Glory!

Yet, I could tell when someone didn't believe me. Their response. The way they looked at me. You know that "look" I am talking about—as if you are crazy.

One time, I called a friend and started to tell her about something I'd experienced and was in awe over. She quickly cut me off and started talking about something else. That day, I came to understand that not everyone has the same relationship with Christ.

Another dear friend of mine—one who always gave me support and acted as an amazing mentor—said to me, "Alison, some things are intimate with you and God. You don't have to tell people everything He speaks to you." She was right. Even though I enjoyed sharing, I could also be excited that some things are just between Him and me.

It will be in the last days, says God, that I will pour out my spirit on all flesh. Your sons and your daughters will prophesy. Your young men will see visions. Your old men will dream dreams. Acts 2:17

I kept reminding myself God remained in control. I only wanted our family to live where He intended. We would make no decision without Him in it.

God spoke to my heart again. *Stop looking for everything that you want in a house and start looking for me.* I realized the home we were meant to be in would not look like what I thought.

I told my husband that I suspected God might be calling us to Nashville, and we needed to be ready if He did. When we initially started looking at houses, we restricted our search to the area in our children's school district.

One day, a friend of mine sent me a picture of a house she'd seen on the market. I skimmed over it at first because it didn't really jump out at me. For some reason though, my mind kept returning to that house. I told Robbie that I was going to ride out and look at it. As I approached the location, mountains came into view. Such beautiful scenery. The land around the house was amazing. I called our realtor right then, and I asked to look at the house.

She made an appointment for us the following week. The yard and outside of the home took my breath away. Before I even entered the house, I knew this was the one. Originally a barn, the house sat in a valley with mountains behind it.

It wasn't what I'd been looking for, but it was definitely different. We would need to change some things, but I said, "God, if this is the one, I am all for it."

There were three offers on the table. The seller could only counter one. Did God intend this? I let the decision be His and didn't worry myself about it. They came back to us with a counteroffer that we could agree to, and knowing God was in it, we purchased the house.

As I sit here at my desk right now, writing this book, I am still in awe of the beauty and the peace we have here. I thank God daily for His mercy, His grace, and His blessings in our lives. He knew exactly what we needed.

For my thoughts are not your thoughts, neither are your ways my ways, declares the Lord. As the heavens are higher than the earth, so are my ways higher than your ways and my thoughts than your thoughts. Isaiah 55:8-9

CHAPTER 7

Rejection Isn't Always a Bad Thing

We must come to understand that when things do not work out in our favor, it is for our own good. Rejection, at times, is for our benefit. Do you ever think, in those times when we're late, or the car breaks down, or our plans go array, God is protecting you? From what, we may never know. I can look back on my life and see where He protected me many times by not letting me have my way. He rerouted me from heartache, disappointment, financial difficulties—and no doubt, from things I don't even know about.

One of the hardest things I've come to accept is that His way is far better than mine. I have to trust in all things that He will protect me and guide my every step. He will never forsake me.

And the Peace of God, which transcends all understanding, will guard your hearts and your minds in Christ Jesus. Philippians 4:7

When you feel rejected and disappointed, remember that God says His peace will guard your hearts and your minds. There is nothing greater than the peace of God.

It is so easy for our minds to get carried away when our hearts get broken. All the "whys and what ifs" try to creep in on us.

I believe God brings us to isolation for a purpose. It is Him working inside us with no distractions.

As I sit here writing this book—definitely not qualified—I know God has asked me to do this. My grammar is terrible. I used to hate to read and write, and now I have found a passion for it.

Isn't it something how God sometimes calls us to do the very thing that we feel most uncomfortable with? I argued with Him many times that I didn't think He picked the right one to do this. He just kept reminding me that I needed to do this.

It hasn't been easy. There have been times I wanted to stop. My love for Jesus outweighs all of that. I would do anything for His glory, not mine. I promised Him that I would be obedient, and I want to fulfill that.

For from him and through him and for him are all things. To him be the Glory forever! Amen. Romans 11:36

How can one go from rejected to redeemed? My answer is that forgiveness is key. You have to choose to not be a victim. I am living proof that God can get you through anything—and you can be redeemed.

I have forgiven the rejection from loved ones. I am grateful for all the suffering I have been through. Without it, I could not have seen Jesus. I would not have felt the need for Him as I do.

We must forgive people and that is not an easy thing—nor is it a one-time thing. For all the people who say I have joined a club that no one wants to be a part of, I say I joined the "Jesus Club." My child stood before Jesus before I did. My child is more alive than I am. But this mother will be reunited with her again one sweet day, and as her mother, I chose to be a warrior and not a victim of grief.

Because God gave His only son to die on the cross for our sins at Calvary, He gave us a choice. A choice to believe in Him and to pick up our cross and follow Him so that we can have eternal life with Him and all of our loved ones. Because of his sacrifice and our salvation, we live to live again. As I mentioned before, Brooke is more alive than we are here on Earth. I have always said, she just passed, not died, meaning she lived and lives again in the Kingdom now, instead of here on Earth.

I pray that every one of you goes from feeling rejected to redeemed. I pray that you all rise up and become warriors, not victims. I pray that you find Jesus as I have. I pray that you laugh again and find joy in life, as the loved ones who have gone before us would want us to do. I thank each and every one of you for taking the time to read this book, and I pray that it leads you to the only Savior who can save and heal us.

In closing, I leave you with one of my favorite scriptures and words from an old hymn:

You will seek me and find me when you seek me with all your heart. I will be found by you, declares the Lord and will bring you back from captivity. Jeremiah 29:13-14

When I think of the goodness of Jesus, and all he has done for me. My soul cries out hallelujah thank God for saving me!

Brooke, age 13

Brooke, age 14

Our family, 2021

"My Saving Grace" Ornament

"Bringing Light to the Loss" Ornament

"How I Survived" Painting

The Brooke Butler Memorial Race

The Brooke Butler Memorial Race

The Brooke Butler Memorial Race

The Brooke Butler Memorial Race, 2015

ACKNOWLEDGMENTS

I could not end this book without acknowledging my Way Maker. The reason I am able to share these things with you, and the One who saved me. The One who made all this possible, The Great I Am, my Heavenly Father. Thank you, Jesus.

To my pastor, mentor, and friend, Tasha Cobbs Leonard. Thank you for that little extra push I needed to move forward. For being there for me in a time of need and for your ministry. You are such a great example of God's love and a light to many. Thank you!

To my sweet friends Nikki, Melanie, Heather, Alli, and Joy. Thank you for being there through all the obstacles, struggles, and doubt. For listening to me when I felt like giving up, feeling it was way out of my comfort zone. For all the pep talks and late-night calls. For just being there to listen on the days it was really hard. I love you all.

To my precious friend and photographer, Noel, owner of Violet Noel Photography. Thank you for everything.

To my dear friend, DeLora, thank you for the sweet journal you gave me that I have written my story in.

To my amazing editor, Joan, and my neighbor, Paige, who have both now become my dear friends. Thank you for all the guidance and knowledge you have taught me throughout this process.

To my amazing family for all of your support. Thank you for believing in me. I love you!

ABOUT THE AUTHOR

Alison Butler Robinson is happily married and a mother of five. She has a passion for Jesus and telling the world how He has saved her many times throughout her life. She made a promise to her daughter Brooke to tell her story to the world and how God changed her life. That is the sole reason she became an author. Alison's goal is to help others find Christ so they can also experience freedom and love in all aspects of life.

Made in the USA
Las Vegas, NV
30 September 2023

78357703R00079